MORE PLEASE!

MORE PLEASE!

MY FAMILY RECIPES YOU'LL - LOVE - TO COOK AND SHARE

MANU FEILDEL

WITH *CLARISSA WEERASENA*

MURDOCH BOOKS

SYDNEY · LONDON

CONTENTS

INTRODUCTION

It seems that when you become part of the so-called 'celebrity' club, people want to know about your private life – and in my case, what I eat at home. I'm sure some folks assume I feast on foie gras, oysters and champagne every day, and much as I love the idea, the reality could not be more different. The truth is that I'm just like you – I'm a passionate home cook. I like simple food made with good-quality seasonal ingredients.

But this book is not just about my take on family cooking. I am fortunate to share the kitchen with my fiancée Clarissa, who is a fabulous cook and has introduced me to many of her family recipes, which take their inspiration from Malay and Chinese cuisines. We both love food and we love to cook for each other as well as for our family and friends.

This shared love of food and cooking is very special to us, and over the years we've introduced each other to dishes we've grown up with and treasured family recipes we've inherited. I don't think I've ever cooked so much at home (or wanted to!). We are always thinking about our next meal and who's cooking what. And our kids eat what we do. I believe that the sooner you introduce your children to new foods the easier life will be for you. We have one rule with food at home and that is 'taste before you judge'!

Of course there are times when Clarissa doesn't want to cook or I don't want to cook, and times when we both do, but for us it's never a chore. Although I must admit that when Clarissa cooks I do all the prep (I'm just quicker and more organised – goes with the job), but when I cook I do it all. Well, Clarissa does the washing up!

So this book is a snapshot of what we like to eat, whether it's a simple mid-week meal or something a bit fancier for when we have people over. I love Clarissa's beautiful curries and soups, quick stir-fries and fragrant vegetable dishes, just as she craves my famous bolognese sauce, hearty stews and traditional French desserts. (And as you will see from the recipes, we usually make enough for there to be leftovers for another day!)

We hope this eclectic collection of recipes will become a family favourite in your house, always open on the benchtop, ready for you to try a new dish.

STARTERS

A great meal begins with an entrée – it teases and entices the tastebuds for what is to follow. The recipes in this chapter will give you all the inspiration you need, and you'll want to eat them again and again. Luckily, most of them can also be enjoyed as a light lunch.

Baked CHEESE CUSTARD

240 ml (8 fl oz) thin
(pouring) cream

240 ml (8 fl oz) full-cream
(whole) milk

4 sprigs thyme

1 small garlic clove,
lightly crushed

3 eggs

2 egg yolks

sea salt

60 g (2¼ oz/½ cup) grated
comté, gruyère or
emmental cheese

60 g (2¼ oz/¾ cup) grated
parmesan cheese

baby leaf and herb salad,
to serve

This delicate dish combines the flavour of a cheese soufflé with the texture of a creamy, just-set panna cotta. It's a total crowd pleaser. Serve it with a simple salad of baby lettuce leaves lightly dressed with your favourite dressing (see page 200 for a couple of suggestions).

Preheat the oven to 150°C (300°F) and lightly grease four 125 ml (4 fl oz/½ cup) ramekins. Fill the kettle with water and bring it to the boil.

Combine the cream, milk, thyme and garlic in a small saucepan over medium heat until the mixture begins to steam.

Meanwhile, put the eggs and yolks in a medium bowl, season with salt and give them a good whisk. Stir in the cheeses.

Remove the thyme and garlic from the cream. Gradually pour the cream into the egg mixture, whisking constantly. Transfer the mixture to a medium saucepan, return to medium heat and whisk until the cheese is completely melted.

Strain the mixture through a fine sieve into a heatproof jug, then pour evenly into the prepared ramekins. Put the ramekins in a deep roasting tin and pour boiling water into the tin until it reaches about 2.5 cm (1 inch) from the top of the ramekins. Bake for 25–30 minutes, or until the custards are nearly but not quite set – they should jiggle a bit in the middle when gently shaken.

Serve warm or at room temperature with a salad of baby herbs and greens.

My Asian-style MUSSELS

2 kg (4 lb 8 oz) mussels in the shell, cleaned and debearded

2 tablespoons peanut oil

1 lemongrass stem, finely chopped

1 fresh long green chilli, thinly sliced

1 fresh long red chilli, thinly sliced

2 golden shallots, thinly sliced

4 garlic cloves, thinly sliced

1 x 3 cm (1¼ inch) piece ginger, julienned

handful of coriander (cilantro), washed, leaves picked and roots chopped

1 x 400 g (14 oz) tin chopped tomatoes

1 x 270 ml (9½ fl oz) tin coconut milk

Clarissa is the expert in the family when it comes to Asian food but every now and then I like to give it a go. I admit upfront that this mussel dish is far from a traditional Asian recipe but it is my interpretation and, if I say so myself, it is absolutely delicious!

Rinse the mussels and drain well.

Place a large heavy-based saucepan or stockpot over medium–high heat and drizzle in the peanut oil. Add the lemongrass, chilli, shallot, garlic, ginger and coriander root and fry for 3 minutes.

Add the mussels and give the mixture a good stir. Pour in the chopped tomatoes and coconut milk and stir again, then cover and bring to the boil. Cook for 5 minutes, shaking the pan a few times, until all the mussels are open. Discard any un-opened mussels.

Serve garnished with the coriander leaves.

MUSHROOMS *on* Toast

4 large slices sourdough bread

1 tablespoon olive oil

30 g (1 oz) butter

400 g (14 oz) mixed mushrooms (such as enoki, shimeji, oyster, button, swiss brown)

2 garlic cloves, finely chopped

80 g (2¾ oz/⅓ cup) crème fraîche or sour cream

handful of parsley, finely chopped

40 g (1½ oz/½ cup) grated parmesan cheese

Clarissa and I love our mushrooms, and we often make this for breakfast on a lazy weekend. In our experience it's better to use a good variety of mushrooms, as they all have their own flavour and texture to add to the mix.

Toast the sourdough bread and keep warm.

Meanwhile, heat a large frying pan over medium–high heat and add the olive oil and butter. When the butter has melted, add the mushrooms and cook for 4–5 minutes, or until soft and caramelised. Add the garlic and cook for 1 minute, then stir in the crème fraîche or sour cream and cook for a further 3 minutes, or until the mushrooms are lightly coated in the creamy sauce. Stir in some of the parsley, to taste.

To serve, divide the mushroom mixture among the four pieces of toast, sprinkle with a little more parsley and finish with the grated parmesan. Dig in!

Nyonya FISHCAKES

10 pieces of banana leaf, thawed if frozen

steamed rice, to serve (optional)

GROUND PASTE

8 red Asian shallots

5 garlic cloves

5 fresh long red chillies, seeded and sliced (for more heat, leave the seeds in)

10 dried red chillies, soaked in hot water for 30 minutes until softened, then drained

1 x 4 cm (1½ inch) piece galangal

1 x 4 cm (1½ inch) piece turmeric (or 1 teaspoon ground turmeric)

3 lemongrass stems, lower pale part only

2 teaspoons belacan (dried shrimp paste), toasted

FISH PASTE

500 g (1 lb 2 oz) Spanish mackerel fillets, skin removed and pin-boned, cut into small cubes

250 ml (9 fl oz/1 cup) coconut cream

2 eggs, lightly beaten

2 heaped tablespoons glutinous rice flour or ordinary rice flour

6–8 kaffir lime leaves, julienned

1 tablespoon sugar

1 teaspoon sea salt

Clarissa's mum was born in the state of Melaka in Malaysia where Nyonya cuisine is very evident, and she is also of Peranakan descent, which is a blend of Chinese ethnicity and Malay-influenced language and culture. The resulting cuisine combines Chinese, Malay and other influences into a unique blend. These fishcakes (otak-otak) are one of the better-known Nyonya dishes and, let me tell you, they make a truly delectable starter.

To prepare the ground paste, coarsely chop all the ingredients, place in a mortar and pestle and blend to a fine paste.

Transfer to a large bowl. Add the fish paste ingredients and mix well to combine, preferably with your hands so you can ensure all the ingredients are well mixed. Cover with plastic wrap and marinate in the refrigerator for at least 4 hours, preferably overnight.

Cut the banana leaves into 20 cm (8 inch) x 18 cm (7 inch) pieces, then wipe them with a clean damp tea towel (dish towel) to remove any dirt. Carefully wilt the banana leaves over a gentle flame or in a wok of boiling water to soften for about 15 seconds, then pat dry and set aside. If your banana leaves were frozen, you can skip this step.

To prepare the parcels, place a piece of banana leaf on a flat surface and scoop 2–3 tablespoons of the marinated fish filling into the centre. Bring up the two longer sides of the leaf and, with the other hand, fold over the shorter ends to meet in the centre. Secure the parcel with a couple of toothpicks. Repeat with the remaining filling and banana leaves.

Half-fill a large saucepan with water and bring to the boil. Place a steamer basket on top, ensuring it fits snugly to avoid any loss of steam and making sure the bottom of the steamer sits well above the water line in the saucepan. Working in two batches (if needed) arrange the parcels in the basket in a single layer and steam for 10–15 minutes, or until cooked to your liking.

For a light smoky flavour, rather than steam the parcels, grill them on a hot barbecue for 5 minutes on each side.

Serve the fishcake parcels on their own or with steamed rice.

SARDINE Rillettes

2 x 106 g (3¾ oz) tins sardines in olive oil, most of the oil drained off

50 g (1¾ oz/⅓ cup) pine nuts, toasted

1 spring onion (scallion), finely chopped

2 tablespoons finely chopped tarragon

100 g (3½ oz) cream cheese

sea salt and freshly ground black pepper

toasts or crispbreads, to serve

I think this might be the easiest, quickest and cheapest recipe in this book, but it's definitely better than tinned baked beans on toast! Great for a little canapé with drinks, or you could serve it as a flavour-packed light lunch. Sometimes the simple things really are the best.

Place the sardines in a medium bowl and mash with a fork until they are broken up but still have a few chunks.

Add the pine nuts, spring onion, tarragon and cream cheese and mix until well combined. Taste and season with salt and pepper, if needed.

To serve, spoon the sardine rillettes into a bowl (or back into the tin for a funky presentation). Serve with toasts or crispbreads.

VEGETABLE *and* ANCHOVY FRITTERS WITH *spicy tomato* DIPPING SAUCE

40 g (1½ oz) dried anchovies

180 g (6½ oz) plain (all-purpose) flour

30 g (1 oz) self-raising flour

½ large red onion, coarsely diced

1 garlic clove, crushed

⅛ teaspoon ground turmeric

150 g (5½ oz) green cabbage, finely shredded

½ small carrot, grated

1 fresh long red chilli, finely chopped

2 teaspoons sea salt

½ teaspoon sugar

canola or vegetable oil, for deep-frying

DIPPING SAUCE

1 tablespoon tomato sauce (ketchup)

80 ml (2½ fl oz/⅓ cup) chilli sauce

½ garlic clove, crushed

juice of ½ lime

2 teaspoons sugar, or to taste

These golden fritters are so addictive that you won't be able to stop eating them. I say this with absolute confidence, so be sure to make extra! The star ingredient is the dried anchovies (ikan bilis), which are salted, sun-dried anchovies. Buy them from your local Asian grocery store. If you can't find them, you can still make the fritters with a similar quantity of chopped raw prawns (shrimp).

For the dipping sauce, combine all the ingredients in a small jug and give them a good stir. Taste for balance of sweet, spicy, sour and salty and adjust if needed, then set aside until you are ready to serve.

Soak the anchovies in enough warm water to cover for 5 minutes, then drain well through a fine sieve. Working in batches, transfer the anchovies to a mortar and pestle and roughly pound. (Alternatively, place in a food processor and process to a coarse paste.)

Combine the flours in a large bowl. Gradually add 250 ml (9 fl oz/1 cup) of water and mix to a thick paste with your hands, removing any lumps as you go. Add the onion, garlic, turmeric, cabbage, carrot and chilli and mix well, then stir in the anchovies, salt and sugar. The batter should now be very thick.

Place a large wok over high heat, pour in the oil for deep-frying until just over one-third full and heat to 180°C (350°F), or until a cube of bread dropped in the oil browns in 15 seconds. Use a small ladle to scoop up large tablespoons of batter and gently place them in the oil, using a spoon to scrape it off the ladle. You want to cook about four or five fritters at a time. Fry the fritters for 1–2 minutes, or until they start to turn golden brown, then gently flip them over and cook for a further 30 seconds, making sure the fritters don't stick to each other. If they seem to be browning too quickly, reduce the heat and allow a little time for the oil to cool slightly before adding the next batch.

Once cooked, remove the fritters with a slotted spoon or spider and drain on a paper-towel-lined plate. Keep warm while you cook the rest, then serve hot with the dipping sauce.

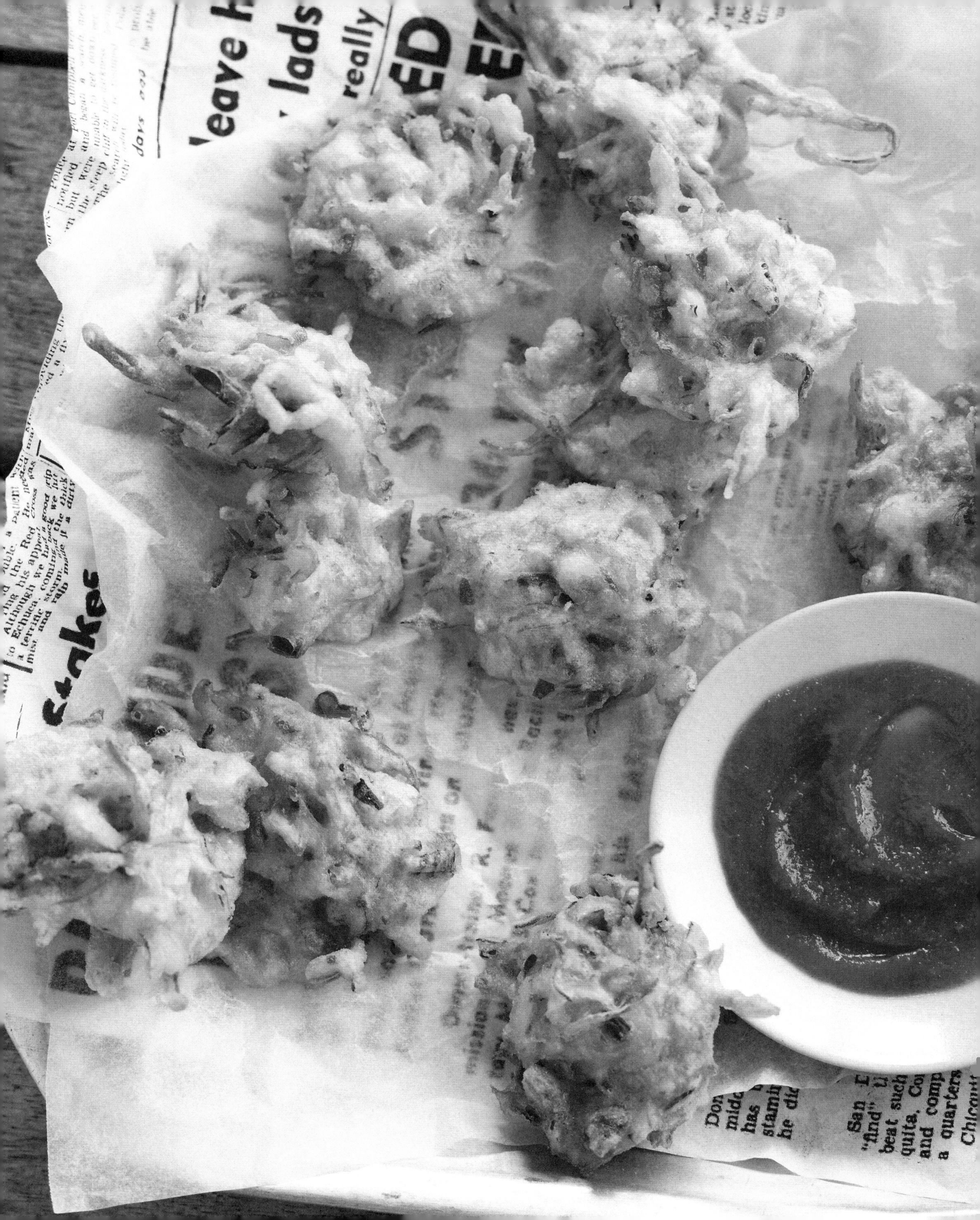

MY Easy SALMON TERRINE

melted butter, for brushing

300 g (10½ oz) salmon fillet, skin removed and pin-boned

2 egg whites

ice cubes

300 ml (10½ fl oz) thin (pouring) cream

200 g (7 oz) smoked salmon, coarsely chopped

1 tablespoon finely chopped tarragon

1 tablespoon finely chopped chervil

1 tablespoon snipped chives

½ teaspoon sea salt

½ teaspoon cayenne pepper

1½ tablespoons olive oil

micro herbs, to garnish (optional)

Mayonnaise or Aïoli (see page 201) and thin slices of toasted baguette or crispbreads, to serve

Terrines can sometimes be a bit labour-intensive but this one couldn't be simpler. It makes a great starter if you have a group of friends coming for dinner, and can also be served as a canapé with drinks.

Preheat the oven to 150°C (300°F). Brush the inside of a 1 litre (35 fl oz/4 cup) terrine mould with melted butter.

Cut the salmon fillet into large chunks. Put them in a food processor with the egg whites and blend for 5 minutes, or until very smooth.

Fill a large bowl with ice. Scrape the salmon paste into a medium bowl and set it over the bowl of ice. Stir in the cream, smoked salmon, herbs, salt, cayenne pepper and olive oil and keep mixing until you reach a mayonnaise-like consistency.

Pour the salmon mixture into the prepared mould. Place the mould in a deep roasting tin and pour boiling water into the tin to come about two-thirds of the way up the sides of the mould. Bake for 20–25 minutes, or until the blade of a small knife comes out clean. Remove the terrine from the oven and leave in the mould to cool completely.

Garnish with micro herbs, if you like. Serve with mayonnaise or aïoli (or even a cocktail sauce) and thin baguette toasts or crispbreads.

Chinese-style OMELETTE

5 eggs

½ teaspoon sea salt

pinch of freshly ground white pepper

pinch of sugar

1 tablespoon soy sauce

60 ml (2 fl oz/¼ cup) peanut or vegetable oil

1 large brown onion, cut into thin wedges

2 Chinese sausages (lap cheong), thinly sliced

1 spring onion (scallion), finely sliced on the diagonal

sliced fresh red chilli, to garnish (optional)

Every cuisine has its own version of the omelette: the English, the French, the Spanish all have one, and so do the Chinese, and this is it! You really can't go wrong with this foolproof recipe. The omelette is usually offered as an accompaniment to other dishes but we also eat it just as it is.

Put the eggs, salt, pepper, sugar and soy sauce in a medium bowl and beat until combined.

Heat a wok or medium non-stick frying pan over high heat, add the oil and heat until slightly smoking. Add the onion and cook for 3–4 minutes, or until slightly golden. Toss in the Chinese sausage and cook for 2–3 minutes, or until crispy.

Spread the onion and sausage evenly over the base of the wok or pan, pour in the egg mixture and tilt the pan to spread evenly, if required. Cook for 1 minute, then carefully turn the omelette over and cook for a further 1 minute, or until golden. Slide onto a plate, garnish with spring onion and chilli (if using) and serve immediately.

MORE PLEASE!

PORK SAUSAGE *and* MUSTARD *in* BRIK PASTRY

4 pork and fennel sausages

8 sheets of brik pastry

100 ml (3½ fl oz) melted butter

thyme leaves, to garnish
(optional)

mixed salad, to serve
(optional)

MUSTARD SAUCE

1½ tablespoons olive oil

30 g (1 oz) butter

2 golden shallots, finely chopped

2 garlic cloves, finely chopped

80 ml (2½ fl oz/⅓ cup)
dry white wine

150 ml (5 fl oz) Brown chicken
stock (see page 197)

100 ml (3½ fl oz) thin
(pouring) cream

50 g (1¾ oz) dijon mustard

30 g (1 oz) wholegrain
dijon mustard

1 thyme sprig, leaves picked
(optional)

sea salt and freshly ground
black pepper

I devoured this dish during my travels near the French town of Troy, which is famous for its andouillettes (pork tripe sausages). Tripe is not to everyone's taste so I have replicated the recipe with friendly pork and fennel sausages instead. Matched with a rich mustard sauce, it's amazingly delicious.

Preheat the oven to 220°C (425°F). Grease a large flat baking tray and line with baking paper.

For the mustard sauce, heat the olive oil and butter in a large heavy-based frying pan over medium heat. When the butter starts to foam, add the shallot and garlic and cook for 2–3 minutes, or until just soft. Pour in the white wine, increase the heat to medium–high and simmer for 3–4 minutes, or until the liquid has reduced by half. Pour in the stock and cream and simmer for 7–8 minutes, or until it reaches a thick sauce consistency. Whisk in both mustards and the thyme, and season to taste with salt and pepper. Set aside.

Heat a frying pan or barbecue plate over high heat and cook the sausages for 4–6 minutes, or until just cooked. You want to give them a nice charred flavour. Allow to cool, then cut them into 1 cm (½ inch) thick rounds.

Place a sheet of brik pastry on your work surface, brush with melted butter and place a second sheet on top. Arrange one-quarter of the sausage slices in the centre and spoon over about one-quarter of the sauce. Carefully fold two sides in and then the two other sides to form a square. If needed, brush with a little more butter to help seal the edges. Invert onto the prepared tray and repeat with the remaining pastry and filling to make four parcels in total. Brush the tops with a little more butter and bake for 5–10 minutes, or until golden.

Garnish with thyme leaves (if using) and serve just as they are, or with a mixed salad. If you have any sauce left over, serve it in a small jug on the side.

ASPARAGUS *with* LIGHT HOLLANDAISE

4 egg yolks

60 ml (2 fl oz/¼ cup) white wine

sea salt

200 ml (7 fl oz) Clarified butter (see page 202)

juice of ½ lemon

200 ml (7 fl oz) thickened (whipping) cream

4 bunches of green or white asparagus, ends trimmed

It's no accident that some recipes are called classics. This asparagus dish, for example, is very simple, but so delicious. Enjoy it as a starter, as a side with a piece of fish, or even for breakfast. Make it in spring when asparagus is plentiful and at its seasonal best.

Half-fill a saucepan with water and bring it to a gentle simmer. Combine the egg yolks, wine and a pinch of salt in a heatproof bowl that fits perfectly on the saucepan without the bowl touching the water. Whisk for 8–10 minutes, or until the whisk leaves a trail and the mixture is thick and creamy.

Remove from the heat and tip out the water. Place the bowl of egg mixture back on the saucepan off the heat and gradually whisk in the clarified butter until the sauce is the consistency of mayonnaise. Whisk in the lemon juice.

Whip the cream until soft peaks form, then gently fold it into the hollandaise. Reserve in a warm spot until you are ready to serve.

Blanch the asparagus in a saucepan of salted boiling water for 3–4 minutes, or until tender but still firm to the bite and bright in colour.

To serve, divide the asparagus spears among four plates, or put them all on one serving dish, and spoon over the sauce.

THE *best* CHEESE FONDUE

1 loaf sourdough

1 garlic clove, halved

500 ml (17 fl oz/2 cups) dry white wine

1 tablespoon cornflour (cornstarch), blended with 1 tablespoon water

200 g (7 oz) emmental cheese, grated

200 g (7 oz) gruyère cheese, grated

200 g (7 oz) swiss cheese, grated

pinch of freshly grated nutmeg

freshly ground white pepper

Originally from the French Alps, cheese fondue has to be the most famous cheese dish of all time. What can be more comforting, more delicious than dipping bite-sized pieces of crusty bread into hot melted cheese after skiing through the mountains? My answer? Nothing. Even if you haven't been skiing beforehand!

A few hours before you are ready to serve, cut the bread into bite-sized cubes and set aside. This will make the bread harden slightly, making it easier to skewer.

Rub the bottom of a cast-iron fondue pot or small saucepan with the cut sides of the garlic, then discard the garlic. Add the wine and bring to the boil over high heat, then reduce the heat to medium.

Stir the cornflour blend into the wine, then gradually add the grated cheeses, stirring constantly with a wooden spoon for 10–15 minutes, or until the cheese has melted and the mixture has thickened. Don't let it boil, and make sure the bottom does not burn – reduce the heat if necessary. Season to taste with nutmeg and pepper.

Serve with the bread cubes and fondue forks, keeping the fondue warm while you eat. If the fondue becomes too thick, just stir in a little more white wine. Bon appétit!

WEEKNIGHT
Meals

Weeknight meals don't have to be a chore, and they certainly don't have to be complicated. Some of the recipes included here need a longer cooking time than others, but if you make a big batch with plenty of leftovers, you'll have a steady supply of flavoursome meals on hand for nights when you really don't want to cook.

BURGUNDY FISH *and* WHITE WINE STEW SERVES 4

1½ tablespoons olive oil

200 g (7 oz) speck bacon,
cut into lardons

1 brown onion,
finely chopped

4 garlic cloves,
lightly crushed

20 button mushrooms

4 thyme sprigs

4 tarragon sprigs,
plus extra to garnish

4 x 500 g (1 lb 2 oz) whole
snapper or other white fish,
cleaned, head and tail removed,
cut into 4 cutlets

sea salt and freshly ground
black pepper

500 ml (17 fl oz/2 cups)
dry white wine

250 ml (9 fl oz/1 cup)
Fish stock (see page 198)

30 g (1 oz) butter, softened

30 g (1 oz) plain
(all-purpose) flour

200 ml (7 fl oz) thin
(pouring) cream

1 egg yolk

boiled kipfler potatoes
or steamed rice,
to serve

I'm sure everyone knows about the famous French dish, Boeuf Bourguignon. Well, this recipe is based on a similar recipe from Burgundy, which is pretty much the same but the beef has been replaced with freshwater fish, and the red wine with white wine. I've reworked it here to feature beautiful Australian seafood.

Place a large heavy-based saucepan over medium heat and drizzle in the olive oil. Add the bacon, onion and garlic and cook for 2–3 minutes. Add the mushrooms, thyme and tarragon and cook, stirring, for 3 minutes.

Season the fish with salt and pepper, add to the pan and cook for 3 minutes. Pour in the white wine. Bring to the boil and flambé. To do this, light a long match and ease it down to the surface of the liquid, without actually touching it. Remove the match as soon as the alcohol ignites and allow it to burn off. (You can skip this step if it seems a bit daunting.) Pour in the stock and simmer for 10 minutes, then remove the fish pieces and set aside in a warm place.

Blend the butter and flour in a small bowl. Increase the heat to high and bring the liquid to the boil, then simmer until reduced by half. Pour in half the cream and return to the boil, then gradually whisk in the butter and flour mixture until thickened to the right sauce consistency (not too thick but not too thin either). Season to taste with salt and pepper.

Take the pan off the heat and whisk in the remaining cream and the egg yolk. Return the fish pieces to the sauce.

Garnish with a little extra tarragon and serve with your choice of potatoes or rice. Remember there are bones in the fish, so take care to eat around them. Enjoy.

Paper Bag CHICKEN

12 dried shiitake mushrooms

4 chicken Marylands
(leg quarters), skin on,
each cut into 3 pieces
(ask your butcher to do
this for you)

vegetable oil, for oiling

6 spring onions (scallions),
white parts halved

peanut oil, for deep-frying

steamed rice, to serve

MARINADE

1 teaspoon Chinese
five-spice powder

2 teaspoons karamel masakan

2½ teaspoons caster
(superfine) sugar

3 teaspoons Ginger juice
(see page 210)

2 teaspoons sesame oil

2 teaspoons oyster sauce

1 tablespoon soy sauce

½ teaspoon sea salt

2 teaspoons Chinese
rice wine

½ teaspoon freshly ground
white pepper

Clarissa used to love watching her grandmother making this, as the process was so intriguing. She used a sewing machine to create parcels out of baking paper, and passed them on to Clarissa's cousin Celina, who was eagerly waiting to fill them with the aromatic chicken. Things got very exciting when the parcels were fried in hot oil, as they puffed up like they were going to explode (they don't, by the way!).

Here we just use staples to keep the parcels together, but do keep count of how many of them you use on each side so when you take them apart you don't leave any behind.

Rehydrate the dried shiitake mushrooms in a bowl of boiling water for 30 minutes. Drain and squeeze to remove the excess liquid, then trim and discard the tough stalks.

To make the marinade, combine all the ingredients in a large bowl. Add the chicken pieces and mushrooms and toss well to coat, then leave to marinate for about 15 minutes.

Cut 12 large (about 30 cm/12 inch) squares of baking paper. Spread a little oil on each square of paper, then place a piece of the chicken, a piece of spring onion and a shiitake mushroom in the centre.

Fold the paper over and crease the edge closest to you three times to enclose the filling. Secure with a few staples (remember to count them), then fold and staple the two open ends in the same way. Repeat with the remaining paper, chicken, spring onion and mushrooms.

Pour peanut oil into a large stockpot or heavy-based saucepan to a depth of 4 cm (1½ inches) and heat over high heat. The oil is ready when a wooden chopstick dipped in the oil starts to bubble or when it reaches 180°C (350°F) on a kitchen thermometer.

Working in batches of three or four, place the chicken parcels in the oil and cook for 5 minutes, then turn and cook for a further 3–5 minutes, or until cooked through, depending on the size of the chicken piece inside. The bags will puff up and you should be able to see the marinade caramelising inside the paper. Remove from the oil with a spider, slotted spoon or tongs and rest for 5 minutes before opening. Cover and keep warm while you cook the remaining parcels.

Open the parcels and serve the chicken with its cooking juices and steamed rice.

My SPAGHETTI BOLOGNESE

SERVES 4

90 ml (3 fl oz) extra virgin olive oil

250 g (9 oz) minced (ground) beef

250 g (9 oz) minced (ground) pork

150 ml (5 fl oz) white wine

100 g (3½ oz) speck bacon or pancetta, finely diced

1 brown onion, finely chopped

1 carrot, finely diced

1 celery stalk, finely diced

3 garlic cloves, finely chopped

1 x 400 g (14 oz) tin chopped tomatoes

400 ml (14 fl oz) Beef stock (see page 198)

150 ml (5 fl oz) milk

sea salt and freshly ground black pepper

400 g (14 oz) spaghetti or other pasta

grilled bread, to serve (optional)

This is probably every kid's favourite meal and it's no different for my son Jonti – he just loooves it. It does take a long time to cook but I think that is the secret to its success: the longer you cook it, the better it will taste. I usually make a big batch and freeze the leftovers for an easy weeknight meal.

Heat half the olive oil in a large frying pan over medium–high heat. When the oil is hot, add the beef and pork and stir with a wooden spatula; at the same time, press down on the meat to break up any lumps. Keep stirring the meat until it is nicely caramelised, about 3–5 minutes, then pour in the white wine. When it starts to boil, reduce the heat to low and simmer until the wine has almost evaporated.

Meanwhile, place a large frying pan over medium–high heat and pour in the remaining oil. When hot, add the speck or pancetta and fry for 1–2 minutes, then add the onion, carrot and celery and cook for about 4 minutes. Add the garlic and cook for another minute.

Now add the vegetable mixture to the meat and pour in the tomatoes and stock. Bring to the boil, then reduce the heat to low and cook, covered, for 1 hour, stirring occasionally.

Remove the lid and cook for another hour, or until the liquid has thickened and reduced by one-third.

Stir in the milk, then taste and season if necessary. Simmer for 10–15 minutes (or longer if you have time, as it will only get tastier with long, slow cooking).

Cook the pasta following the packet directions until al dente. Drain and serve with a generous helping of bolognese sauce and some grilled bread, if you like.

EGGPLANT STUFFED *with* BEEF RAGOUT

SERVES 4

2 small–medium eggplants (aubergines)

170 ml (5½ fl oz/⅔ cup) olive oil

1 teaspoon thyme leaves

4 garlic cloves, finely chopped

sea salt and freshly ground black pepper

250 g (9 oz) minced (ground) beef

250 g (9 oz) minced (ground) pork

150 ml (5 fl oz) white wine

1 brown onion, finely chopped

1 carrot, finely diced

1 celery stalk, finely diced

400 ml (14 fl oz) Beef stock (see page 198)

1 x 400 g (14 oz) tin chopped tomatoes

70 g (2½ oz/¼ cup) tomato paste (concentrated purée)

100 g (3½ oz/1¼ cups) grated parmesan cheese

handful of parsley, coarsely chopped (optional)

If you feel that you've had too many carbs lately, this a great substitute: replace the spaghetti with eggplant and voilà! I'm not saying it's necessarily healthier, but who cares when it tastes this good?

Preheat the oven to 190°C (375°F) and line a baking tray with baking paper.

Cut the eggplants in half and mark a crisscross pattern in the flesh with a small knife. Drizzle each half with 1 tablespoon of olive oil, sprinkle over the thyme leaves and a little bit of the chopped garlic (reserving most of it to use later in the ragout), then season with salt and pepper. Place the eggplant halves on the prepared tray and roast for 25–30 minutes, or until just cooked. Set aside.

Heat 2 tablespoons of olive oil in a large frying pan over medium heat. When the oil is hot, add the beef and pork and stir with a wooden spatula; at the same time, press down on the meat to break up any lumps. Keep stirring the meat until it is nicely caramelised, about 4–5 minutes, then pour in the white wine. When it starts to boil, reduce to a simmer and cook until the wine has almost evaporated.

Meanwhile, put a large heavy-based saucepan over medium–high heat and pour in the remaining olive oil. When it's hot, add the onion, carrot and celery and cook for 3–4 minutes, then add the remaining garlic and cook for another minute. Add the meat mixture, stock, tinned tomatoes and tomato paste and bring to the boil, then reduce the heat to low, cover and cook for 1 hour, stirring occasionally.

Remove the lid and cook for a further 45–60 minutes, or until it reaches the right consistency – not too saucy but also not too dry.

Put a good spoonful of ragout on the cut side of each eggplant and sprinkle the parmesan evenly over the top. Place under a very hot grill (broiler) for 3–5 minutes, or until the cheese is melted and golden brown. Serve with a sprinkling of fresh parsley, if using.

Any leftover ragout may be stored in an airtight container in the fridge for up to 5 days, or frozen for 3–4 months.

BEEF CHEEK *and* PEARL BARLEY SOUP

SERVES 4–6

2 large beef cheeks,
each cut into 4 pieces

sea salt and freshly ground
black pepper

2 tablespoons olive oil

2 brown onions, finely diced

2 garlic cloves, crushed

250 ml (9 fl oz/1 cup) red wine

750 ml (26 fl oz/3 cups)
Beef stock (see page 198)

1 bay leaf

1 tablespoon rosemary leaves

5 thyme sprigs

1 leek, cut into 1 cm
(½ inch) cubes

2 carrots, cut into 1 cm
(½ inch) cubes

2 parsnips, cut into 1 cm
(½ inch) cubes

100 g (3½ oz) button
mushrooms, sliced

120 g (4¼ oz) pearl barley

handful of parsley,
coarsely chopped

grilled bread,
to serve (optional)

You may need to put a little more preparation time into this recipe than for some other soups but it is definitely worth the effort. The combination of pearl barley and soft, gelatinous beef cheek in a strongly flavoured stock is very moreish, and wonderfully warming during the chilly winter months.

Season the beef cheeks with salt and pepper.

Place a large heavy-based saucepan or stockpot over medium–high heat and drizzle with half the olive oil. When hot, brown the beef in small batches, making sure it is well caramelised. Remove the meat from the pan and reserve.

Drizzle the remaining oil into the pan, add the onion and garlic and sauté for 2–3 minutes, or until the onion has softened.

Pour in the red wine and simmer until the liquid has reduced by half. Return the beef to the pan and add the stock, bay leaf, rosemary, thyme and 1 litre (35 fl oz/4 cups) of water. Cover with a lid and bring to the boil, then reduce the heat to low and simmer for 2–2½ hours, or until the beef is soft and tender and falls apart easily. Stir well to shred the beef and distribute it through the soup. Add the vegetables and barley, then cover and simmer for a further 25–30 minutes, or until the vegetables and barley are soft.

To serve, ladle the soup into warm bowls and garnish with parsley. Serve with grilled bread, if you like.

Steamed Stuffed SQUID

200 g (7 oz) minced (ground) pork

1½ tablespoons peanut oil

1 brown onion, finely chopped

1 carrot, finely chopped

6 tinned water chestnuts, drained and finely chopped

3 large squid tubes, cleaned

shredded spring onion (scallion), to garnish (optional)

steamed rice, to serve

MARINADE

½ teaspoon fish sauce

½ teaspoon sea salt

½ teaspoon sesame oil

½ teaspoon sugar

½ teaspoon soy sauce

2 teaspoons cornflour (cornstarch)

pinch of freshly ground white pepper

The combination of meat and seafood may seem a little unusual but it is often used in Asian cooking. This squid and pork recipe is something Clarissa's mum came up with – it's a lovely clean-tasting dish that's full of flavour.

To make the marinade, combine all the ingredients in a large bowl. Add the pork and mix together well.

Place a small frying pan over medium heat and drizzle in the peanut oil. When hot, add the onion and sauté gently until just translucent. Set aside to cool, then incorporate the onion, carrot and water chestnut into the pork mixture.

Fill the squid tubes with the stuffing, taking care not to overfill them as the stuffing will expand as it cooks. Carefully seal each squid tube with a couple of toothpicks.

Arrange the squid in a shallow heatproof dish that will fit in a bamboo steamer.

Fill a saucepan or wok with 1–1.5 litres (35–52 fl oz/4–6 cups) of water. Make sure the steamer basket fits snugly in (or over) the pan and isn't in danger of tipping over. Also ensure the bottom of the steamer sits above the water line and won't become submerged. Cover the pan or wok and bring the water to a simmer.

Steam the squid for 10–12 minutes, or until it turns an opaque white colour. As it cooks, keep an eye on the water level and add more if it starts to boil dry.

Transfer the squid tubes to a clean plate and let them rest for 10 minutes so the stuffing and its juices have time to settle.

To serve, cut the tubes into 2 cm (¾ inch) thick slices and finish with a good drizzle of the cooking juices. Garnish with spring onion, if you like, and serve with steamed rice.

Tomato Prawn CURRY

3 lemongrass stems,
pale part only, bruised
and coarsely chopped

1 x 3 cm (1¼ inch) piece ginger,
coarsely chopped

3 brown onions,
coarsely chopped

3 garlic cloves, crushed

60 ml (2 fl oz/¼ cup)
sunflower oil

2 pandan leaves,
tied together in a knot

2 tablespoons fish curry powder
(I like Baba's brand)

4 roma (plum) tomatoes,
seeded and cut into 1 cm
thick (½ inch) pieces

250 ml (9 fl oz/1 cup)
coconut milk

1 kg (2 lb 4 oz) raw tiger prawns
(shrimp), peeled and deveined
(if you like, or leave them whole)

1 teaspoon sea salt

1 teaspoon sugar

½ teaspoon soy sauce

½ teaspoon fish sauce

1 teaspoon lime juice

steamed rice and lime wedges,
to serve

This is one of the many dishes Clarissa's mum taught her to cook and it's so easy to make. We usually use whole prawns with the heads on, as this gives a greater depth of flavour to the sauce, but you can peel them if you prefer.

Place the lemongrass, ginger, onion and garlic in a mortar and pestle or the bowl of a food processor and pound or process to a paste.

Heat a large frying pan or wok over medium heat and add the sunflower oil. Once smoking, add the lemongrass paste and pandan leaves and sauté for 3–5 minutes, or until fragrant and caramelised.

Blend the curry powder with 2–3 tablespoons of water to make a paste. Add to the wok and cook for 5 minutes, or until fragrant. Add the tomato and fry for 3–5 minutes, then pour in the coconut milk and 250 ml (9 fl oz/1 cup) of water and simmer for 2 minutes.

Add the prawns, salt, sugar, soy sauce and fish sauce and cook, stirring occasionally, for 7–8 minutes, or until the prawns are almost cooked. Season with lime juice, cover and leave to rest for 5 minutes to finish cooking.

Serve with steamed rice and lime wedges.

JOHN DORY *with* CHORON SAUCE

SERVES 4

4 x 200 g (7 oz) John Dory fillets, skin on and pin-boned

sea salt and freshly ground black pepper

60 ml (2 fl oz/¼ cup) olive oil

60 g (2¼ oz) butter

your choice of greens, to serve

CHORON SAUCE

2 golden shallots, finely chopped

1 tablespoon crushed black peppercorns

1 tablespoon dried tarragon

100 ml (3½ fl oz) white wine

2½ tablespoons white wine vinegar

1 tomato

6 egg yolks

250 ml (9 oz/1 cup) warm Clarified butter (see page 202)

sea salt

1 teaspoon tomato paste (concentrated purée)

2 tablespoons finely chopped chervil

2 tablespoons finely chopped tarragon

I'm sure by now you are well aware of my love affair with sauces, and this one is no exception. I love to serve it with my favourite fish, John Dory, but it would work well with any white-fleshed fish. It's pretty much a béarnaise sauce with the addition of tomato, which brings a beautiful sweetness to the dish.

For the choron sauce, place the shallot, peppercorns, dried tarragon, wine and vinegar in a medium saucepan and bring to the boil over high heat. Reduce the heat to medium–low and simmer for 8–10 minutes, or until the liquid has almost evaporated. Set the reduction aside to cool completely.

Meanwhile, cut an X in the base of the tomato and put in a small saucepan of simmering water for 60–90 seconds, or until the skin begins to come away from the flesh. Plunge into cold water and gently peel away the skin. Cut into quarters and remove the seeds, then finely chop the flesh. Set aside.

Combine the egg yolks and cold reduction in a heatproof bowl. Place over a saucepan of simmering water, ensuring the bowl fits snugly to create a bain-marie (water bath), but doesn't touch the surface of the water, and whisk until thick and fluffy.

Remove the bowl from the saucepan. Gradually whisk in the warm clarified butter, pouring it in a thin stream until emulsified. Season with salt to taste.

Press the sauce through a fine sieve into a bowl, then stir in the tomato paste, diced tomato, chervil and tarragon. Reserve in a warm spot until you are ready to serve.

Pat the John Dory fillets dry with paper towel and season with salt and pepper on both sides.

Place a large non-stick frying pan over medium–high heat and drizzle in the olive oil. Add the fillets, skin side down, and apply a little bit of pressure with the help of a fish slice or spatula to stop the skin from curling up. Cook for 4–5 minutes, or until the flesh is two-thirds cooked. Flip the fillets over. Add the butter to the pan and, when it starts to foam, spoon it over to baste the skin for 1 minute, or until the fish is cooked to your liking.

To serve, place the fillets on warmed plates and serve with a good dollop of choron sauce and a side of your favourite greens. Finish with a grinding of pepper, if liked.

Malaysian Fried CHICKEN

SERVES 4

6 garlic cloves,
peeled and left whole

5 small red Asian shallots,
halved and skin removed

1 x 4 cm (1½ inch) piece ginger,
coarsely chopped

2 lemongrass stems,
pale part only, bruised and
coarsely chopped

2 tablespoons canola oil
(optional)

1 tablespoon lime juice,
plus extra to serve (optional)

2 teaspoons soy sauce,
plus extra to serve (optional)

1 egg, lightly beaten

1 tablespoon chilli powder

3 teaspoons curry powder

½ teaspoon ground cumin

½ teaspoon whole aniseeds

½ teaspoon ground coriander

35 g (1¼ oz/¼ cup) plain
(all-purpose) flour

1 tablespoon sea salt,
plus extra to serve

3 teaspoons caster
(superfine) sugar

4 chicken Marylands
(leg quarters), skin on,
each cut into 3 pieces
(ask your butcher to do
this for you)

canola or vegetable oil,
for deep-frying

All I can say about this chicken is that it's lip-smacking, finger-licking good!
It is served in all 'mamak' stalls (outdoor food stalls) in Malaysia, which are open
until the wee hours of the morning – perfect for a late supper after a big night
out at a club. It's great as an appetiser, but it's usually served as a main with
Coconut rice (see page 92).

Put the garlic, shallot, ginger and lemongrass in a food processor and process to
a fine paste, adding canola oil if required to reach a paste consistency. Stir in the
lime juice, soy sauce and egg.

Combine the spices, flour, salt and sugar in a large bowl, then whisk in the garlic
mixture until combined. Add the chicken pieces and mix until each piece is well
coated in the marinade. Cover with plastic wrap and marinate at room temperature
for at least 1 hour.

Heat the oil in a deep-fryer or saucepan to 180°C (350°F), or until a cube of bread
dropped in the oil browns in 15 seconds. Working in batches of three pieces at
a time (or more, depending on the size of your fryer or pan), carefully ease the
chicken into the oil and cook for 7–9 minutes, or until crisp, golden brown and
cooked through (smaller pieces will cook in 7 minutes, while larger pieces will
need an extra minute or two). Drain well on a plate lined with paper towel. Cover
with foil to keep warm while you cook the remaining pieces. Before you start each
new batch, make sure you have fished out all the bits and pieces floating in the oil.

Sprinkle with extra sea salt and serve with extra soy sauce or lime juice, if liked.

JAPANESE TOFU *with* MINCED PORK

SERVES 2–3

200 g (7 oz) minced
(ground) pork

4 dried shiitake mushrooms

boiling water, for soaking

3 x 150 g (5½ oz) tubes
Japanese egg tofu

peanut or canola oil,
for shallow-frying

35 g (1¼ oz/¼ cup)
cornflour (cornstarch)

3–4 garlic cloves,
finely chopped

1 teaspoon oyster sauce

¼ teaspoon karamel masakan

¼ teaspoon caster
(superfine) sugar

¼ teaspoon sea salt

2 teaspoons cornflour
(cornstarch), extra,
blended with 1 tablespoon water

sea salt and freshly ground
black pepper (optional)

shredded spring onion
(scallion), to garnish

MARINADE

¼ teaspoon sea salt

1 teaspoon sesame oil

1 teaspoon soy sauce

dash of freshly ground
black pepper

1 teaspoon Chinese rice wine

Tofu is such a misunderstood food, largely I think because of its reputation for having a wobbly texture, which is not to everyone's taste. But if you get over that hurdle and cook it the right way, I promise you'll be pleasantly surprised. Remember, tofu comes in various forms: hard, soft, spongy, dried, fried … the list goes on. The tofu in this recipe is made from eggs and soy beans, and is available in the refrigerator section of Asian grocery shops. I dare you to try it!

To make the marinade, combine all the ingredients in a medium bowl. Add the pork and mix to combine. Set aside.

Rehydrate the dried shiitake mushrooms in a bowl of boiling water for about 30 minutes, or until soft. Drain, then remove and discard the tough stalks and finely chop the caps.

Cut each tofu tube in half, then carefully remove the tofu from the packaging by gently squeezing the ends and letting the tofu slide out. Cut each half into three or four equal pieces, then drain on paper towel to remove any excess liquid if required.

Heat a large frying pan over high heat, add the oil to a depth of 1 cm (½ inch) and when slightly smoking, reduce the heat to medium. Lightly dust the tofu with cornflour. Gently lift up each tofu disc with a spatula and shallow-fry in small batches for 1–2 minutes on each side until golden. Once cooked, the tofu should be lightly crisp on the outside and still soft and smooth on the inside. Set aside on a serving dish.

Place a clean frying pan over medium heat. When hot, add 2 tablespoons of oil and the garlic and stir-fry until fragrant and very lightly golden. Add the mushrooms and stir-fry for about 1 minute.

Add the marinated pork and stir-fry for 2–3 minutes, or until nearly cooked. Pour in the oyster sauce, karamel masakan, sugar and salt and stir to combine. Bring to the boil, then stir in the cornflour paste and cook for 2–3 minutes, stirring constantly, until the sauce has thickened slightly. Season with salt and pepper, if desired.

To serve, drizzle the pork mixture over the tofu and garnish with spring onion.

Manu

Clarissa's mum's CHICKEN CURRY

SERVES 4

vegetable oil, for deep-frying, plus 1–2 tablespoons extra if needed

3 potatoes, quartered

6–7 red Asian shallots, depending on size

4 garlic cloves

1 x 4 cm (1½ inch) piece ginger

50 g (1¾ oz) curry powder (I like Baba's brand)

125 ml (4 fl oz/½ cup) canola or sunflower oil

1 cinnamon stick

2 star anise

4–5 cloves

1 kg (2 lb 4 oz) chicken Marylands (leg quarters), skin on, each cut into 4 pieces (ask your butcher to do this for you)

2 sprigs curry leaves

250 ml (9 fl oz/1 cup) coconut cream

3 teaspoons lime juice

1 teaspoon caster sugar

1½ teaspoons sea salt, plus extra to taste

steamed jasmine rice, to serve

As you can see, Clarissa uses ready-made curry powder in this all-time family favourite, which isn't uncommon in Malaysian households. There are so many around and, quite frankly, most of them are pretty good. One word of advice, though: for the sake of authenticity, check the label and make sure it is made in either Malaysia or Singapore. If you prefer not to deep-fry the potato, just add the uncooked potato to the pan halfway through the chicken cooking time.

Heat the vegetable oil in a deep-fryer or saucepan to 200°C (400°F), or until a cube of bread dropped in the oil browns in 5 seconds. Deep-fry the potato for 8–10 minutes, or until cooked, crisp and golden. Set aside on paper towel to drain.

Meanwhile, place the shallots, garlic and ginger in a mortar and pestle or small food processor and pound or process to a fine paste, adding 1–2 tablespoons of oil if required to help loosen the paste.

Stir 3–4 tablespoons of water through the curry powder and mix until it reaches a paste consistency, adding a little more water if required.

Heat the canola or sunflower oil in large frying pan over medium–high heat. Add the cinnamon, star anise and cloves and toast for 15–20 seconds. Add the shallot paste and fry for 5–7 minutes, or until fragrant and translucent. Stir in the curry paste and fry for 2–3 minutes.

Add the chicken and stir to coat well, then cook for 3–5 minutes, turning occasionally, until it has begun to take on a golden colour. Add the curry leaves and 375 ml (13 fl oz/1½ cups) of water and bring to the boil, then reduce the heat to low and simmer for 20 minutes.

Add the fried potatoes and mix to combine. Stir in the coconut cream and bring to a simmer, then cook for another 10–15 minutes, or until the chicken is tender. Add lime juice, sugar and salt, to taste.

Serve with steamed jasmine rice.

MY MOROCCAN-STYLE COUSCOUS
with LAMB CUTLETS

SERVES 4

2 tablespoons olive oil,
plus extra for drizzling

1 large brown onion,
finely chopped

1 tablespoon sea salt,
plus extra to taste

½ teaspoon freshly ground
black pepper, plus extra to taste

1 teaspoon ground turmeric

1 teaspoon ground ginger

generous pinch of saffron

2 ripe tomatoes, seeded and
cut into 2 cm (¾ inch) pieces

1 x 400 g (14 oz) tin chickpeas,
rinsed and drained

handful of coriander
(cilantro) stalks, tied to
a bouquet with kitchen string,
plus extra leaves to garnish

1 large sweet potato,
cut into large chunks

300 g (10½ oz) turnips,
cut into 3 cm (1¼ inch) chunks

3 carrots, cut into 4 cm
(1½ inch) chunks

2 fresh long red chillies,
cut in half lengthways

2 small–medium zucchini
(courgettes), cut into 5 cm
(2 inch) long pieces

16 lamb cutlets

1 teaspoon ground cumin

COUSCOUS

200 g (7 oz/1 cup) couscous

1 teaspoon sea salt

2 tablespoons olive oil

This recipe is not a traditional North African couscous but rather my interpretation of one. Same ingredients, same spices, same flavours but a lot quicker to make for a midweek meal, and a great way to introduce your kids to spices.

To make the couscous, preheat the oven to 160°C (315°F). Spread out the couscous in a large ovenproof dish and pour over 250 ml (9 fl oz/1 cup) of cold water. Mix together and leave to stand for 30 minutes. Use a fork to separate the grains of couscous until light, fluffy and well separated. Add the salt and olive oil and mix until the couscous grains are nicely coated. Cover with foil and heat through in the oven for 25–30 minutes, then remove and cover with a tea towel to keep warm until you are ready to serve.

Meanwhile, place a large heavy-based saucepan or flameproof casserole dish over medium heat and drizzle in the olive oil. Add the onion, salt, pepper, spices and half the tomato and cook, stirring, for 8–10 minutes.

Add the chickpeas and 1.5 litres (52 fl oz/6 cups) of water. Bring to the boil, then reduce the heat to medium–low and drop in the coriander bouquet. Add the sweet potato, turnip, carrot and chilli to the broth and bring back to the boil. Reduce the heat and simmer, covered, for 35–40 minutes.

Remove and discard the coriander bouquet and continue to cook, covered, for a further 20 minutes.

In the meantime, spoon about 150 ml (5 fl oz) of the broth into a separate casserole dish or saucepan and place over medium heat. Add the zucchini, then cover and cook for 20 minutes, flipping the zucchini halfway through. (I cook the zucchini separately because it becomes very fragile once cooked and might break if you cook it in the broth with the rest of the vegetables.)

Add the zucchini and remaining tomato to the rest of the vegetables and season to taste with salt and pepper if needed. Keep warm until required.

Heat a large frying pan or chargrill plate over very high heat. Season the cutlets with cumin and salt and pepper to taste. Drizzle a little extra olive oil into the pan and, when smoking, add the cutlets and cook for 2 minutes on each side or until nicely caramelised. Allow to rest for a few minutes.

To serve, spoon a pile of couscous into the centre of a large serving plate and rest the cutlets all around. Garnish with fresh coriander leaves and serve with the vegetable stew on the side.

OXTAIL and CARROT STEW

SERVES 4

60 ml (2 fl oz/¼ cup) olive oil

60 g (2¼ oz) butter

1 oxtail, cut into 6 cm
(2½ inch) thick pieces

sea salt and freshly ground
black pepper

12 golden shallots,
peeled and left whole

1 kg (2 lb 4 oz) carrots,
each cut into 4 pieces

2 brown onions, diced

1 leek, diced

1 celery stalk, diced

4 garlic cloves, crushed

1 tablespoon plain
(all-purpose) flour

1½ tablespoons thyme leaves

2 bay leaves

350 ml (12 fl oz) red wine
(preferably cabernet sauvignon
or shiraz)

1 litre (35 fl oz/4 cups)
Beef stock (see page 198),
or as needed

coarsely chopped parsley,
to garnish

pasta or mashed potato,
to serve

My mother often cooked this quintessential mid-week French winter dish for us when we were growing up. It's warm and filling, and great served simply with pasta or potato mash.

Preheat the oven to 160°C (315°F).

Place a large flameproof casserole dish over medium–high heat, add half the olive oil and butter and allow the butter to melt.

Meanwhile, season the oxtail pieces with salt and pepper.

When the butter starts to turn light brown, add the oxtail and cook on each side for 2–3 minutes, or until well caramelised. Transfer to a plate and reserve.

Heat the remaining olive oil and butter in the casserole dish, add the shallots and carrot and cook for 3 minutes, or until golden brown. Add the onion, leek, celery and garlic and cook for 2 minutes, or until soft.

Stir in the flour, then return the oxtail to the dish, along with the thyme, bay leaves and red wine. Increase the heat to high so the mixture boils and reduces by half, then pour in enough stock to just cover. Bring back to the boil, stirring to make sure the flour doesn't stick to the bottom of the dish. Cover with a lid, place in the oven and cook for 2½–3 hours, or until the meat just falls off the bone.

Garnish with parsley and serve with pasta or mashed potato.

Malaysian SPICY CHICKEN

1 kg (2 lb 4 oz) chicken Marylands (leg quarters), skin on, each cut into 3–4 pieces (ask your butcher to do this for you)

100 ml (3½ fl oz) canola or vegetable oil

1 large brown onion, cut into rings

1 fresh green chilli, thickly sliced on the diagonal

1 fresh red chilli, thickly sliced on the diagonal

steamed rice, to serve

SEASONING

1 teaspoon sea salt

1 teaspoon sugar

SAUCE

1 tablespoon karamel masakan

1 tablespoon sugar, plus extra if needed

1 teaspoon sea salt, plus extra if needed

2 teaspoons white vinegar, plus extra if needed

Another traditional Nyonya dish from Clarissa's mum, this is also her grandfather's favourite dish. This is a great example of how a few simple ingredients can really pack a punch with flavour.

Put the chicken pieces in a large bowl.

Combine the seasoning ingredients in a small bowl, then sprinkle over the chicken and rub into the flesh. Set aside for 30 minutes.

For the sauce, put all the ingredients and 250 ml (9 fl oz/1 cup) of water in a medium bowl and mix together well. Set aside until required.

Heat a medium–large wok over high heat until very hot, then pour in 80 ml (2½ fl oz/⅓ cup) of the oil. Once the oil is almost smoking, add the onion and half the red and green chilli and stir-fry for 30–60 seconds, or until the onion and chilli begin to take on a golden colour. Remove with a slotted spoon or spider and drain well on paper towel.

Add the chicken to the onion-infused oil and stir-fry over high heat for about 5–7 minutes.

Add the sauce (take care as the oil may spit) and cook for 5 minutes, tossing the chicken occasionally to coat it in the liquid. Reduce the heat to low, cover and cook gently for 15–20 minutes, or until the chicken is tender, stirring occasionally. Remove the lid, add the remaining chilli and oil and stir to combine. Add more sugar, salt or vinegar, to taste.

Top with the crispy onion and chilli mixture and serve with steamed rice.

Jonti's FAVOURITE MINCE

SERVES 4

2 large potatoes,
cut into 1 cm cubes

1 tablespoon vegetable oil

1 large brown onion, diced

500 g (1 lb 2 oz) minced
(ground) pork or beef

2 tablespoons karamel masakan

1 teaspoon light soy sauce

1 tablespoon white vinegar

1 teaspoon sugar

½ teaspoon sea salt,
plus extra if needed

1 teaspoon freshly ground
black pepper, plus extra
if needed

200 g (7 oz) frozen peas

steamed rice or spaghetti,
to serve

My son Jonti can't get enough of this dish – the very mention of mince meat gets him bouncing off the walls in excitement! Well, maybe not that dramatic, but he does love it. As you can imagine, this is something Clarissa cooks for Jonti all the time. It's great served with steamed rice or even spaghetti.

Bring a saucepan of salted water to the boil, add the potato and simmer for 5–7 minutes, or until just tender. Drain and set aside.

Heat the oil in a large frying pan over medium heat, add the onion and cook for 5 minutes, or until translucent. Add the pork or beef and stir-fry for a few minutes until browned, breaking up any lumps with a wooden spoon as you go.

Combine the soy sauces, vinegar, sugar, salt and pepper, then pour over the meat mixture and stir well. Gently fold in the drained potato and cook for 2 minutes.

Add the frozen peas and cook for another minute until the peas are thawed. Adjust the seasoning if necessary, and serve with rice or spaghetti.

My Moroccan-style
CHICKEN TAGINE

1 teaspoon ground coriander

1 teaspoon ground cumin

1 teaspoon ground turmeric

1 teaspoon ground ginger

½ teaspoon cayenne pepper

½ teaspoon smoked paprika

1 teaspoon sea salt

½ teaspoon freshly ground black pepper

6 chicken Marylands (leg quarters), each cut into 3 pieces (ask your butcher to do this for you)

2 tablespoons olive oil

4 brown onions, finely chopped

3 garlic cloves, finely chopped

100 g (3½ oz) fresh dates, pitted

150 g (5½ oz) dried apricots

coarsely chopped coriander (cilantro) leaves, to garnish

Couscous (see page 64), to serve

I love Moroccan food and have a particular soft spot for tagines. While this dish takes its inspiration from traditional North African cooking it doesn't have to be cooked in a tagine. It's a more accessible way for the family to enjoy an aromatic, gently spiced meal that could otherwise take hours to prepare.

Combine all the spices, salt and pepper in a large bowl and add the chicken pieces. Mix well, making sure that all the chicken is well coated with the spice blend, then set aside.

Heat the olive oil in a large heavy-based frying pan or enamelled cast-iron casserole dish over medium heat. Add the onion, cover with a lid and cook for 10 minutes, stirring occasionally, until it is soft and translucent. Add the garlic and chicken and cook for 5–7 minutes, turning the chicken occasionally.

Pour over 300 ml (10½ fl oz) of water, or enough to cover the chicken pieces, and bring to the boil. Reduce the heat to low, cover with a lid and gently simmer for 20 minutes.

Add the dates and apricots and cook for a further 20 minutes, stirring occasionally, until the meat is nicely cooked and starting to fall off the bone. Taste and adjust the seasoning, adding salt as desired.

Sprinkle with coriander and serve with couscous.

BEEF *and* DARK BEER STEW

2 tablespoons olive oil

4 x 5 mm (¼ inch) thick slices of speck bacon (about 160 g/5¾ oz)

1 kg (2 lb 4 oz) braising beef (preferably oyster blade), cut into 5 cm (2 inch) cubes

sea salt and freshly ground black pepper

2 brown onions, cut into 1 cm (½ inch) thick slices

4 golden shallots, cut into thick rings

3 garlic cloves, crushed

50 g (1¾ oz) dark brown sugar

100 ml (3½ fl oz) red wine vinegar

1 tablespoon plain (all-purpose) flour

600 ml (21 fl oz) dark beer

500 ml (17 fl oz/2 cups) Beef stock (see page 198)

4 thyme sprigs

2 bay leaves

2 tablespoons dijon mustard

4 slices ginger cake (store-bought is fine) or day-old bread

I think most Aussie blokes would love the sound of this stew: beef and beer! The French cannot take the credit for the recipe, as it is more of a Belgian dish, but we enjoy it all the same. It's an interesting combination of flavours, particularly the dark beer, which is an integral part of the recipe. To be honest, I'm not really sure where the addition of ginger cake comes from – it's just the way this stew has always been cooked. Unexpected certainly, but I can promise you it really works!

Preheat the oven to 160°C (315°F).

Place a large cast-iron casserole dish or ovenproof saucepan over medium–high heat and drizzle in 1 tablespoon of olive oil. When hot, add the bacon and fry on each side for about 2 minutes, or until slightly caramelised. Transfer to a plate and reserve.

Increase the heat to high. Season the beef with salt and pepper, then add to the pan in two or three batches and sear in the bacon fat, stirring occasionally, for 3–4 minutes, or until all sides are caramelised. Remove and set aside with the bacon.

Reduce the heat to medium and drizzle the remaining olive oil into the pan. Throw in the onion and shallot and cook for 3 minutes, then add the garlic and cook for 1 minute. Add the brown sugar and cook slowly until a caramel starts to form. Deglaze with the vinegar, then give the onion mixture a good stir and return the beef and bacon to the pan. Sprinkle over the flour and give it another good stir, pour in the beer and stock, then add the thyme and bay leaves. Stir and bring to the boil, then reduce the heat to low so the mixture just simmers.

Dollop the mustard evenly onto the ginger cake slices and place on top of the stew. Transfer to the oven and bake for 2½–3 hours, or until the beef is tender. Season with salt and pepper to taste.

Serve just as it is, or with your favourite potato dish, such as Duck-fat potatoes with garlic and rosemary (see page 146).

Red CHICKEN

1 x 1.7 kg (3 lb 12 oz) chicken

2 teaspoons sea salt,
plus extra if needed

2 teaspoons ground turmeric

250 ml (9 floz/1 cup) vegetable oil

1 cinnamon stick

1 star anise

3 cloves

2 cardamom pods

1 x 2 cm (¾ inch) piece ginger,
thinly sliced

2 garlic cloves, thinly sliced

1 large red onion, cut into rings

3 tomatoes, cut into wedges

100 ml (3½ fl oz) tomato
sauce (ketchup)

1 tablespoon sugar,
plus extra if needed

steamed rice, to serve

SPICE PASTE

10 dried long red chillies,
halved lengthways and seeded

boiling water, for soaking

6–7 red Asian shallots

1 x 4 cm (1½ inch) piece galangal

2 lemongrass stems,
pale part only

1 x 4 cm (1½ inch) piece ginger

3 garlic cloves, peeled

Often served at weddings, this is another classic Malay dish. It has a wonderful blend of sweet, spicy and tangy flavours, and every time Clarissa makes it we agree we should eat it more often! If you are cooking for children you can either reduce the amount of chilli or leave it out altogether.

Cut the chicken into 12 pieces, breaking it down so you have two legs, two wings, two thighs and two breasts, cutting each breast into three pieces.

Combine the salt and turmeric and massage it into chicken pieces, then set aside for 30 minutes.

Meanwhile, to make the spice paste, soak the dried chillies in boiling water for 10 minutes, then drain and slice. Roughly chop the shallots, galangal, lemongrass, ginger and garlic. Place in a food processor with the drained chillies and blend until a smooth paste forms. Set aside.

Heat the oil in a large deep frying pan over medium–high heat. Add the chicken pieces and shallow-fry for 5 minutes, turning to brown on all sides. Remove from the pan and place in a large bowl. Depending on the size of your pan, you may need to do this in two batches.

Reduce the heat to medium–low and tip in the spice paste and whole spices. Fry for 10 minutes, stirring regularly and taking care not to burn the paste. Add the ginger, garlic and onion and cook for 2 minutes. Stir in the tomato wedges, tomato sauce and sugar.

Return the chicken and any juices to the pan and stir to coat with the spice mixture. Add 250 ml (9 floz/1 cup) of water and bring to the boil over high heat, then reduce the heat, cover and simmer for 45 minutes, stirring once or twice during this time. Taste and season with salt or sugar if needed.

Serve with steamed rice.

Pork-stuffed ZUCCHINI CURRY

SERVES 4

300 g (10½ oz) minced (ground) pork

4 large or 6 small zucchini (courgettes)

6 golden shallots

4 garlic cloves

1 x 5 cm (2 inch) piece ginger, coarsely chopped

50 g (1¾ oz) curry powder

125 ml (4 fl oz/½ cup) grapeseed oil

1 cinnamon stick

2 star anise

4–5 cloves

2 curry leaf sprigs

sea salt

250 ml (9 fl oz/1 cup) coconut cream

1–2 teaspoons sugar

1–2 teaspoons lime juice

freshly ground black pepper (optional)

steamed rice, to serve

MARINADE

1 teaspoon curry powder

pinch of sea salt and freshly ground black pepper

We usually make this dish with snake gourd, but it can be really hard to find them here so to make life easier I've replaced them with zucchini. It has the same texture and it actually doesn't taste that different from the gourd. This curry goes really well with Turmeric okra (see page 154) and steamed rice.

Place the pork and marinade ingredients in a medium bowl and mix well.

Trim the top and tail from each zucchini then, using an apple corer, hollow out the seeds from both ends. Stuff each zucchini with the pork mixture and set to one side.

Put the shallot, garlic and ginger in a food processor with a couple of tablespoons of water and blitz until puréed.

Blend the curry powder with 100 ml (3½ fl oz) of water to make a paste. Set aside.

Heat the oil in a large heavy-based saucepan over medium–high heat, add the stuffed zucchini and fry for 8–10 minutes, or until lightly browned and the skin has bubbled, turning occasionally. Set the zucchini aside on a plate.

Add the cinnamon, star anise and cloves to the wok of hot oil and toast for 30 seconds. Reduce the heat to medium, add the shallot purée and gently fry for 5 minutes, or until translucent. Add the curry paste and fry for 5 minutes, then add the curry leaves and 500 ml (17 fl oz/2 cups) of water. Bring to the boil, then reduce the heat and simmer for 10–12 minutes. Season with a little salt to taste.

Return the stuffed zucchini to the pan. Bring to the boil, then reduce the heat and simmer for a further 10–12 minutes, or until just tender. Pour in the coconut cream, reduce the heat to very low and simmer for 5–10 minutes, making sure it does not come back to the boil otherwise the coconut cream will split. Season with sugar and lime juice to taste, and salt and pepper, if necessary.

Serve with steamed rice.

MORE PLEASE!

NOODLES and RICE

Noodles and rice are staple ingredients in most Asian cuisines, and are on constant rotation in our household. The recipes that follow can be enjoyed by all the family, although in some cases you may want to tone down the chilli if you are feeding children too. It's all a matter of personal taste.

HOKKIEN NOODLES *with* PORK *and* PRAWNS

SERVES 4–6

250 g (9 oz) pork scotch fillet, thinly sliced

1 bunch choy sum

1 kg (2 lb 4 oz) hokkien noodles

100 ml (3½ fl oz) peanut or vegetable oil

3 small garlic cloves, finely chopped

12 raw prawns (shrimp), peeled and deveined, tails intact

250 ml (9 fl oz/1 cup) Chicken stock (see page 196)

1 tablespoon soy sauce, plus extra to taste

1 large brown onion, diced

sea salt, to taste

2 fresh long red chillies, thinly sliced (optional)

MARINADE

1 tablespoon Chinese rice wine

1 teaspoon freshly ground white pepper

½ teaspoon sea salt

¼ teaspoon sugar

2 tablespoons oyster sauce

2 tablespoons cornflour (cornstarch)

What's not to like in this crowd-pleasing recipe? Easy to cook and even easier to eat, it's everything you want in a noodle dish. As with all stir-fries, make sure you have all the ingredients and sauces prepared and close to your wok before you start cooking.

To make the marinade, combine all the ingredients in a bowl. Add the pork and stir to coat thoroughly, then cover and set aside for 30 minutes.

Wash the choy sum well, then separate the leaves from the stalks and cut into 5 cm (2 inch) pieces.

Bring a kettle of water to the boil. Put the noodles in a colander set over a large heatproof bowl and pour over the boiling water to rinse. Drain thoroughly and set aside.

Heat a large wok over high heat and add 2 tablespoons of oil. When the oil is starting to smoke, add the pork and marinade and stir-fry for 2 minutes. Add the garlic and prawns and stir-fry for another minute. Add the choy sum stalks and toss to combine, then pour in the chicken stock and half the soy sauce and cook for 2 minutes. Add the choy sum leaves and stir until wilted. Transfer to a bowl or plate and set aside.

Heat the remaining oil in the wok over high heat. When the oil is smoking, add the onion and stir-fry for 3–4 minutes, or until it is lightly golden. Add the noodles, spreading them evenly across the wok, and leave to crisp slightly at the bottom. Drizzle over the remaining soy sauce and stir-fry for a few seconds.

Add the pork and prawn mixture and toss to combine. Season with salt and extra soy sauce to taste, and serve garnished with fresh chilli, if desired.

PUMPKIN *and* LEMON THYME RISOTTO

SERVES 4–6

500 g (1 lb 2 oz) butternut pumpkin (squash)

60 ml (2 fl oz/¼ cup) olive oil

about 20 lemon thyme sprigs

3 garlic cloves, crushed

sea salt and freshly ground black pepper

1 litre (35 fl oz/4 cups) Chicken stock (see page 196)

1 brown onion, chopped

250 g (9 oz/1¼ cups) arborio rice

150 ml (5 fl oz) white wine

juice of 1 lemon

100 g (3½ oz) butter, cut into cubes

50 g (1¾ oz) parmesan cheese, finely grated

Roasting the butternut pumpkin first intensifies the flavour and makes it quite sweet, and puréeing it gives the risotto an extra creamy consistency. You can serve this as a vegetarian main meal if you use vegetable stock instead, but it also makes a great accompaniment to a piece of fish or chicken.

Preheat the oven to 160°C (315°F).

Cut the pumpkin in half lengthways and scoop out the seeds. Drizzle each half with 2 teaspoons of olive oil, and sprinkle a few sprigs of lemon thyme and a crushed garlic clove over each half. Season with salt and pepper.

Place the pumpkin on a baking tray and roast for 1 hour, or until the flesh is very soft. Remove from the oven and cool a little, then scrape the flesh from the skin and blend in a food processor until smooth. Set aside.

Pour the stock into a saucepan and bring to the boil. Reduce the heat to medium and keep it at a low simmer.

Meanwhile, place a large deep frying pan or cast-iron casserole dish over medium heat and drizzle in the remaining olive oil. Add the onion and remaining garlic clove and cook for 2–3 minutes, or until the onion is translucent but hasn't taken on any colour.

Add the rice and stir until all the grains have been coated with oil, then add the wine and eight or nine sprigs of lemon thyme and let it reduce for 1–2 minutes. Reduce the heat to low, add one or two ladles of stock and cook, stirring occasionally, until the liquid has been absorbed. Repeat this step with the remaining stock until the rice is just cooked or slightly 'al dente'.

To finish, add the lemon juice and pumpkin purée. When it's nicely incorporated stir in most of the butter and parmesan. Season to taste with salt and pepper.

To serve, immediately spoon the risotto into warmed shallow bowls and garnish with the remaining butter and parmesan and the last sprig or two of lemon thyme.

Black Hokkien NOODLES

SERVES 6–8

1 x 500 g (1 lb 2 oz) piece
boned pork belly

2 tablespoons peanut oil

1 kg (2 lb 4 oz) hokkien noodles

3 small golden shallots,
finely chopped

6 garlic cloves, finely chopped

12 medium raw prawns (shrimp),
peeled and deveined

200 g (7 oz) piece fishcake,
thinly sliced

¼ small Chinese cabbage
(wom bok), shredded

about 125 ml (4 fl oz/½ cup)
karamel masakan

2–3 tablespoons light soy sauce

125 ml (4 fl oz/½ cup) Chicken
stock (see page 196)

3 teaspoons sugar,
plus extra if needed

3 teaspoons freshly ground
white pepper, or to taste

sea salt (optional)

1 teaspoon cornflour
(cornstarch) blended with
1 tablespoon water

Cooked sambal chilli
(see page 208), to serve

PORK MARINADE

1 tablespoon soy sauce

1 teaspoon sea salt

1 teaspoon sesame oil

dash of freshly ground
white pepper

We regularly make our version of this popular Malaysian Chinese dish at home, and not just for dinner – we often tuck into a bowl as a late-night snack. If you prepare all the ingredients in advance it takes only minutes to cook. The crispy pork pieces can be prepared a couple of days ahead and stored in the fridge.

Cut the skin and fat off the pork belly and reserve. Thinly slice the belly flesh and place in a separate bowl.

To make the pork marinade, combine all the ingredients in a bowl. Pour over the belly slices, toss to combine and set aside for 30–60 minutes to marinate.

Cut the reserved pork belly skin and fat into 1 cm cubes. Put in a wok with the peanut oil over medium–low heat and render the fat for 30–35 minutes, or until the little pork pieces are crispy and slightly golden. Take care, as the hot oil will spit. Remove the pork pieces from the oil using a slotted spoon or spider and drain on a plate lined with paper towel. Drain the rendered fat into a heatproof container and refrigerate until required. Set the pork pieces aside until you are ready to serve or, if you have made them ahead of time, store in an airtight container in the fridge until needed.

Bring a kettle of water to the boil. Put the noodles in a colander set over a large heatproof bowl and pour over the boiling water to rinse. Drain thoroughly and set aside.

Before you begin stir-frying, ensure you have all the ingredients prepared and close by.

Heat a wok over very high heat. Add 80 ml (2½ fl oz/⅓ cup) of the reserved pork fat and heat until smoking. Add the marinated pork belly and stir-fry briskly for 1 minute. Add the shallot and garlic and fry for 30 seconds. When just browned, add the prawns and fishcake and stir-fry for 30 seconds. Toss in the Chinese cabbage and stir-fry for a further 30 seconds or so. Add the noodles and quickly toss to combine.

Add the karamel masakan and soy sauce and mix to coat the noodles. Add more karamel masakan if required to adjust the colour and flavour. Add the stock, sugar and white pepper and stir-fry to combine. Taste the sauce and adjust the saltiness and sweetness if necessary to suit your taste.

Stir in the cornflour blend and toss until the sauce has thickened and the noodles are well coated.

To serve, divide the noodles among bowls or plates, spoon over the sauce and garnish with crispy pork pieces. Serve with cooked sambal belacan on the side.

Our FRIED RICE

300 g (10½ oz/1½ cups) jasmine or long-grain rice

4 eggs

pinch of sugar

1 teaspoon freshly ground white pepper

80 ml (2½ fl oz/⅓ cup) peanut oil

1 large brown onion, finely chopped

3 Chinese sausages (lap cheong), cut into cubes, or 250 g (9 oz) streaky bacon, cut into 5 mm (¼ inch) thick strips

8 medium raw prawns (shrimp), peeled and deveined, each cut into 3 pieces

1 tablespoon sea salt

2 teaspoons soy sauce, or to taste

3 spring onions (scallions), pale and green parts separated, thinly sliced on the diagonal

20 g (¾ oz) butter

dash of fish sauce (optional)

I know that there are hundreds of versions of fried rice out there but this version, not surprisingly, has a little French influence: butter! There is a reason this simple ingredient is a chef's secret weapon.

Wash the rice four or five times until the water runs clear. Transfer to a medium saucepan and add 750 ml (26 fl oz/3 cups) of water, ensuring the rice is level so it cooks evenly. Bring to the boil, then reduce the heat to medium and cook for about 5 minutes, or until tunnels form in the rice and most of the water has been absorbed. Take off the heat and set aside, covered, for about 10 minutes to allow the rice to steam through and become fluffy. Remove the lid and run a fork through the rice. (Alternatively, you can use a rice cooker.)

Spread the cooked rice on a baking tray lined with baking paper (this will help the rice cool faster and will also soak up any excess moisture). You can do this up to a day ahead and keep it in the fridge, if you like.

Put the eggs, sugar and a pinch of the white pepper in a bowl and whisk together.

Heat a large wok over high heat and add 1 tablespoon of the oil. When it is smoking hot, pour in the egg mixture. As soon as the egg starts to sizzle, start stirring it as if you are making scrambled eggs. Remove the egg from the wok as soon it's cooked and set aside.

Heat the remaining oil in the wok and wait until it is smoking again, then add the onion and stir-fry until it starts to become translucent. Add the Chinese sausage or bacon and stir-fry for 1–2 minutes.

Sprinkle over the remaining white pepper as you are cooking, then add the prawns and cook for a further 1 minute. Season with salt, then add the cooked rice. Spread the rice around the wok, then let it sit for a few minutes. Don't over-stir the rice at this point – you want it to stick to the wok and crisp up, adding a delicious texture to the dish.

Add soy sauce to taste. If the rice looks a little dry, add hot water 1 tablespoon at a time until it reaches your desired consistency. Toss through the pale part of the spring onion and the cooked egg, then remove from the heat and scatter over the green part of the spring onion.

Quickly mix through the butter to give the rice a flavour boost and a good shine, season with a dash of fish sauce, if you like, and serve.

Grandma-in-law's LAKSA

400 g (14 oz) skinless chicken breast fillets

1 litre (35 fl oz/4 cups) Chicken stock (see page 196)

sea salt, to taste

20 fish balls

200 g (7 oz) piece fishcake, boiled and thinly sliced

800 g (1 lb 12 oz) raw tiger prawns (shrimp)

80 ml (2½ fl oz/⅓ cup) peanut oil

175 g (6 oz) Laksa paste (see page 210)

500 ml (17 fl oz/2 cups) coconut milk

sugar, to taste

250 ml (9 fl oz/1 cup) coconut cream

20 fried tofu puffs, scalded in hot water briefly to remove excess oil

500 g (1 lb 2 oz) egg noodles, blanched in hot water and drained

300 g (10½ oz) vermicelli, soaked in cold water for 30 minutes, then blanched in hot water and drained

200 g (7 oz) bean sprouts

1 Lebanese (short) cucumber, julienned

large handful of Vietnamese mint, coarsely chopped

90 g (3¼ oz/⅓ cup) Sambal belacan (see page 208)

2 limes, cut into wedges

Some say that laksa is the quintessential south-east Asian noodle soup dish. Well let me tell you that this happens to be THE recipe from Clarissa's family that was locked firmly in the vault until this book! With the consent of Clarissa's mother you are now invited to cook this most treasured dish in your own home. Enjoy!

Place the chicken breasts in the bottom of a small heavy-based saucepan – they should fit in a single layer but quite snugly. Cover with the chicken stock and sprinkle over 2 teaspoons of salt. Place over high heat and bring to the boil, then quickly reduce the heat to low and simmer for 10 minutes. Remove from the heat and leave the chicken to poach in the stock, covered, for 10 minutes, or until cooled. Fish out the chicken breasts and roughly shred the meat. Reserve the stock in the pan.

Bring the saucepan of stock to the boil over high heat, add the fish balls and cook for 2 minutes, or until they float to the surface. Remove with a slotted spoon and set aside. Add the fishcake and cook for 2 minutes, then remove and set aside.

Lastly, add the prawns and cook for 3 minutes, or until cooked through. Remove with a slotted spoon and leave to cool slightly, then peel and devein the prawns. Set the prawns aside and reserve the stock – by now it's going to be full of flavour!

Heat the oil in a large heavy-based saucepan, add the laksa paste and fry for a few minutes until fragrant.

Pour in the reserved stock and bring to the boil. Add the coconut milk and salt and sugar to taste, then return to the boil, stirring constantly. Once the broth starts to boil, reduce the heat to low and stir in the coconut cream. Increase the heat just enough to bring the laksa broth to a simmer, add the tofu puffs and stir constantly, turning off the heat just before the broth comes back to the boil.

To assemble, place a little of each type of noodle in serving bowls and top with the shredded chicken, fish balls, fishcake and prawns. Ladle over the hot laksa broth with some tofu puffs and garnish with bean sprouts, cucumber and mint. Serve with sambal belacan and lime wedges on the side.

VERMICELLI, FISH BALL *and* CHICKEN NOODLE SOUP

2 skinless chicken breast fillets

sea salt

16 fish balls

400 g (14 oz) vermicelli, soaked in cold water for 30 minutes

1 teaspoon sugar

freshly ground white pepper

100 g (3½ oz) shredded iceberg lettuce

3 spring onions (scallions), shredded

50 g (1¾ oz) crispy fried shallots

sesame oil, to taste

2 fresh bird's eye chillies, thinly sliced, or to taste

soy sauce, to serve

CHICKEN STOCK

1 kg (2 lb 4 oz) chicken wings

1 x 4 cm (1½ inch) piece ginger, smashed once with a pestle

1 carrot, cut into large chunks

½ brown onion

4 garlic cloves, smashed once with a pestle

Clarissa makes this comforting soup for me all the time – even when I'm not sick! Although the ingredients list may look long, it really isn't hard to make. All you need to do is prepare the elements and assemble them when the stock is ready. Fish balls are made from a ground fish paste and come in a variety of flavours. Look for them in your local Asian grocery store.

To make the chicken stock, place all the ingredients and 2 litres (70 fl oz/8 cups) of water in a large heavy-based saucepan over high heat and bring to the boil. As soon as it's boiling, reduce the heat to medium–low and simmer for 1 hour. Remove from the heat and skim off any impurities, then leave to cool. Once cool, strain through a muslin (cheesecloth)-lined sieve into a clean container. Set aside until needed.

When you're ready to poach the chicken, put the chicken breasts in a small heavy-based saucepan (they should fit snugly in a single layer). Cover with 1 litre (35 fl oz/4 cups) of the chicken stock, reserving the rest of the stock, and sprinkle with salt. Place over high heat and bring to the boil, then immediately reduce the heat to a simmer and gently poach the chicken for 10 minutes. Remove from the heat and let the chicken rest in the stock for another 10 minutes, or until cooled. Fish out the chicken breasts, reserving the stock, and roughly shred the meat.

Transfer the stock to a medium saucepan and bring to the boil over high heat. Add the fish balls and cook for 2–3 minutes. The fish balls will float to surface when cooked – when they do, remove them from the pan and set aside. Reserve the remaining stock.

Bring a kettle of water to the boil. Drain the vermicelli noodles and transfer to a heatproof bowl, then pour over the boiling water and allow them to cook for 1 minute. Remove with a fine-mesh sieve and set aside until required.

Add about 500 ml (17 fl oz/2 cups) of the reserved chicken stock to the stock you cooked the fish balls in, or enough to reach 1.5 litres (52 fl oz/6 cups). Bring to the boil over high heat and season with salt, sugar and pepper to taste.

Divide the noodles, shredded chicken, fish balls, lettuce and spring onion among four bowls. Garnish with fried shallots and pour in enough hot stock to just cover the noodles. Season to taste with a dash of sesame oil and white pepper.

Serve with chilli soaked in soy sauce on the side.

MALAYSIAN COCONUT RICE
with condiments

5 eggs

200 g (7 oz) dried anchovies

60 ml (2 fl oz/¼ cup) canola
or vegetable oil

150 g (5½ oz) raw peanuts,
skin on

pinch of sea salt

1 telegraph (long) cucumber,
halved lengthways then cut into
5 mm (¼ inch) thick slices

Squid sambal (see page 148)
and Clarissa's mum's chicken
curry (see page 62), to serve

COCONUT RICE

400 g (14 oz/2 cups) long-grain
or basmati rice

500 ml (17 fl oz/2 cups)
coconut milk

1 x 3 cm piece ginger,
julienned

1 teaspoon sea salt

1 teaspoon fenugreek seeds

2 pandan leaves,
tied in a knot

There is nothing more Malaysian than coconut rice (nasi lemak). It's traditionally served with sambal and a few garnishes as a breakfast dish, but you can add more substantial accompaniments if you're after a more filling meal. We love it with fried chicken, beef rendang, chicken curry or deep-fried fish (see pages 58, 126, 62 and 129), but it's entirely up to you.

For the coconut rice, rinse the rice in cold water until the water runs clear. Drain well, then tip the rice into a large heavy-based saucepan. Pour in the coconut milk and 375 ml (13 fl oz/1½ cups) of water and place over high heat. Add the ginger, salt, fenugreek and pandan leaves and bring to the boil. Reduce the heat to low, then cover and cook for 20–25 minutes, or until all the liquid has been absorbed. Remove from the heat and set aside for 5 minutes with the lid still on. Fluff with a fork or chopsticks. (If you'd rather use a rice cooker, cook the rice according to the manufacturer's instructions or for 30 minutes until tender.)

Put the eggs in a saucepan large enough to hold them in a single layer and add enough cold water to cover by 2.5 cm (1 inch). Place over high heat and when the water just comes to the boil, remove from the heat and cover. Let the eggs stand in the hot water for about 12 minutes for large eggs (9 minutes for medium eggs; 15 minutes for extra large). Once cool, peel and cut them in half lengthways.

Soak the dried anchovies in a bowl of cold water for 10 minutes, then drain and pat dry with paper towel.

Pour the oil into a small saucepan over high heat. When it is very hot, deep-fry the anchovies in small batches for 2–3 minutes, or until crisp and golden. Remove with a slotted spoon or spider and drain on paper towel. Set aside. Any anchovies you don't eat can be cooled and stored in an airtight container for 1–2 weeks.

Heat a medium frying pan over medium heat, Add the peanuts, then reduce the heat to very low and dry-fry, stirring constantly, until the skin is browned. Sprinkle over a pinch of salt. (If you want to skip this step, you can buy beer nuts and these will do just as well!)

To serve, pack the rice into a small bowl and turn it over in the middle of each dinner plate. Assemble a little portion each of the cucumber, condiments and curries around the rice.

Claypot CHICKEN RICE

6 small dried shiitake mushrooms

500 g (1 lb 2 oz) chicken thigh fillets, preferably with skin on, cut into bite-sized pieces

300 g (10½ oz/1½ cups) long-grain rice

500 ml (17 fl oz/2 cups) Chicken stock (see page 196)

½ teaspoon sea salt

1 Chinese sausage (lap cheong), thinly sliced on the diagonal

1 spring onion (scallion), thinly sliced on the diagonal

2–3 fresh bird's eye chillies, thinly sliced

2–3 tablespoons light soy sauce

juice of 1 lime

MARINADE

1½ tablespoons Ginger juice (see page 210)

1 tablespoon oyster sauce

2 tablespoons light soy sauce

1 teaspoon karamel masakan

2 teaspoons sugar

½ teaspoon sea salt

¼ teaspoon freshly ground black pepper

2 teaspoons sesame oil

1 teaspoon Chinese rice wine

Claypot chicken rice was one of the first dishes Clarissa learnt to cook when she left Malaysia to study in Australia. She missed it so much and couldn't find anywhere that served it so she simply had to make it herself. Needless to say, it's become one of our favourite family meals.

Soak the shiitake mushrooms in boiling water for 20 minutes, or until softened. Drain and squeeze out any excess water, them trim and discard the tough stalks. Cut the mushroom caps in half.

To make the marinade, combine all the ingredients in a medium bowl. Add the chicken pieces and mushrooms and toss to coat. Cover and set aside for 30 minutes.

Rinse the rice until the water runs clear, then drain well. Transfer the rice to a clay pot, wok or medium heavy-based saucepan, add the chicken stock and salt and bring to the boil over high heat. Immediately reduce the heat to medium–low and cook for 10 minutes, or until most of the liquid has been absorbed.

Heat a large frying pan over medium heat and stir-fry the chicken and mushrooms for 3–5 minutes, or until sealed on all sides but not cooked through. Push the chicken pieces into the rice slightly, then drizzle the marinade and mushrooms over the top. Cover the pan with a tight-fitting lid and leave to cook over low heat for 7–10 minutes. Do NOT lift the lid off the pan during this time.

Remove the pan from the heat and set aside, covered, for 10 minutes to allow the chicken to finish cooking. When it's cooked, spoon the chicken and rice into a serving dish. You should have a crunchy crust on the bottom of the pan – this is the best part of the meal!

Heat a small frying pan over high heat and cook the Chinese sausage, stirring occasionally, for 1–2 minutes, or until the sausage is golden. Drain on paper towel.

Serve the rice and chicken hot, garnished with spring onion and Chinese sausage, with a small side dish of chilli mixed with soy sauce and lime juice.

Singapore NOODLES

SERVES 4

150 g (5½ oz) pork fillet, thinly sliced

6 dried shiitake mushrooms

250 g (9 oz) vermicelli, soaked in cold water for 30 minutes

3 eggs

sea salt and freshly ground white pepper

60 ml (2 fl oz/¼ cup) peanut oil

3 garlic cloves, chopped

½ brown onion, sliced into thin wedges

½ large carrot, julienned

8 raw prawns (shrimp), peeled and deveined, tails intact

6 garlic chives, cut into 4 cm (1½ inch) lengths

100 g (3½ oz) bean sprouts, well washed

MARINADE

1 teaspoon freshly ground white pepper

1 tablespoon oyster sauce

2 tablespoons soy sauce

1 teaspoon sesame oil

1 teaspoon sugar

1 teaspoon cornflour (cornstarch)

TO SERVE

2 fresh long red chillies, thinly sliced

lemon juice, to taste

soy sauce, to taste

Singapore noodles are basically the fried rice of noodles. You'll find it at just about every Chinese restaurant or takeaway joint. Here is Clarissa's version of this popular classic, and it's a hit with everyone in the family.

To make the marinade, combine all the ingredients in a large bowl. Add the pork and toss well to coat, then set aside.

Rehydrate the dried shiitake mushrooms in a bowl of boiling water for 30 minutes. Drain, reserving the liquid, then remove and discard the tough stalks and thinly slice the caps.

Cut the softened noodles two or three times into shorter lengths.

Beat the eggs in a bowl with a dash of white pepper and salt.

Heat a non-stick frying pan over low heat and drizzle in ½–1 teaspoon of peanut oil. Pour 2–3 tablespoons of the beaten egg into the pan and swirl to coat – you want it to cover the base of the pan in a thin layer. Cook for 1 minute, or until just cooked through. Remove and repeat with the remaining egg mixture to make about six pancakes in total. Roll up each pancake and cut into thin strips. Set aside.

Once you get to this point, the dish literally takes minutes to cook!

Heat a large wok over high heat and pour in the remaining oil. When it is slightly smoking, add the garlic and onion and stir-fry for 2–3 minutes, or until lightly golden.

Add the pork and stir-fry for 2–3 minutes. Stir in the carrot and mushroom, then the prawns and stir-fry for another 2 minutes.

Stir in 60 ml (2 fl oz/¼ cup) of the reserved mushroom liquid, add the noodles and toss to combine. Cook for 1–2 minutes, or until the noodles are soft, adding a bit more water if necessary. Season with salt and pepper to taste.

Remove the wok from the heat and mix through the chives and bean sprouts.

Divide the noodle mixture among four bowls, top with the egg ribbons and serve with sliced chilli, lemon juice and soy sauce on the side.

For when Friends COME OVER

Although you shouldn't feel you have to work too hard to impress your friends, it's always nice to make an effort. With that in mind, most of the recipes here are quite simple, but we have also included a few 'cheffy' ones for when you want to go all out and knock their socks off.

POACHED FISH MOUSSE *with* PRAWN SAUCE

SERVES 6

500 g (1 lb 2 oz) raw prawns (shrimp)

250 g (9 oz) flathead fillets (or any other white fish fillets), skin removed and pin-boned

3 egg whites

300 ml (10½ fl oz) thin (pouring) cream

1 tablespoon finely chopped chervil, plus extra sprigs to garnish

1½ teaspoons sea salt

olive oil and cayenne pepper, to garnish

fresh baguette, to serve

PRAWN SAUCE

1½ tablespoons olive oil

1 tablespoon tomato paste (concentrated purée)

250 g (9 oz) butter, softened

½ quantity Basic béchamel (see page 204)

200 ml (7 fl oz) thin (pouring) cream

sea salt and cayenne pepper, to taste

This is a very old-school French dish from the city of Lyon, which is considered the capital of French food. The mousse is rich, but also soft and delicate – perfect for a special occasion when you're out to impress.

Peel and devein the prawns. Discard the heads, but reserve the rest of the shells. Set the meat aside for making the mousseline mixture.

For the prawn sauce, start by making a prawn butter. Place a medium saucepan over medium heat and drizzle in the olive oil. Add the reserved prawn shells and cook for 2–3 minutes, stirring frequently until the shells turn red and start to caramelise. Add the tomato paste and cook for another minute. Scrape the shell mixture into a food processor and blend to a paste. Add the butter and blend again until well combined. Scrape the butter mixture back into the saucepan and melt slowly over low heat. Set aside for 30 minutes, then press though a fine sieve into a bowl and refrigerate to set. (The prawn butter will keep well in the fridge for up to a week.)

Meanwhile, place the flathead, reserved prawn meat and egg whites in a clean food processor and pulse until smooth. Tip the paste into a bowl, add the cream and chopped chervil and gently mix to combine. Add the salt, ½ teaspoon at a time, mixing vigorously until the mixture starts to firm up. Cover and refrigerate for at least 1 hour before cooking.

To finish the sauce, warm the basic béchamel in a medium saucepan. Whisk in the cream and 50 g (1¾ oz) of the reserved prawn butter until well combined. Season to taste with salt and cayenne pepper and remove from the heat.

To cook the mousseline, bring a large saucepan of unsalted water to the boil, then reduce to a low simmer. Dip a large metal serving spoon into the simmering water so it's hot then, holding the spoon with the rounded bottom up, place the far edge of the spoon into the mixture and drag it carefully toward you. The mixture should start to curl into a quenelle as you drag, then twist your wrist up to lift it out of the bowl. Dip the spoon and the quenelle in the simmering water (the quenelle should detach itself from the spoon). Repeat to add a second quenelle and cook for 7–8 minutes, gently turning once. Remove the quenelles from the water with a slotted spoon and drain on a clean tea towel (dish towel). Repeat with the remaining mousseline mixture to make six large quenelles in total.

When you're ready to serve, warm the sauce over medium heat until just below simmering point. Pour a generous amount of sauce into six shallow bowls and place a quenelle in the centre of each. Garnish with extra chervil sprigs, a drizzle of olive oil and a pinch of cayenne pepper and serve with a crusty baguette to soak up the last of the béchamel.

LAMB CUTLETS *with* MINT HOLLANDAISE

SERVES 4

1½ tablespoons olive oil

16 lamb cutlets, seasoned with sea salt and pepper

mint sprigs, to garnish

MINT HOLLANDAISE

3 golden shallots, finely chopped

60 ml (2 fl oz/¼ cup) white wine

1½ tablespoons white wine vinegar

1 teaspoon dried mint

1 teaspoon crushed black peppercorns

4 egg yolks

sea salt

250 ml (9 fl oz/1 cup) Clarified butter (see page 202)

1 tablespoon finely chopped mint

juice of ½ lemon

freshly ground black pepper

Hollandaise is the cousin of béarnaise sauce, and both play a very important role in French cuisine. Flavoured with tarragon, béarnaise is terrific with beef, but with lamb the natural choice has to be this rich, creamy hollandaise, enhanced with fresh and dried mint.

To make the hollandaise, combine the shallot, white wine, vinegar, dried mint and peppercorns in a small saucepan over high heat and bring to the boil. Reduce the heat medium–low and simmer for 3–5 minutes, or until most of the liquid has evaporated. Transfer to a heatproof bowl that fits snugly over a saucepan and set aside to cool.

Half-fill the saucepan with water and bring to the boil over high heat. Reduce to a simmer.

Add the egg yolks to the shallot reduction in the bowl, along with a pinch of salt, then rest the bowl over the saucepan, making sure the bottom of the bowl doesn't touch the water, and start whisking. It should foam and then thicken to the consistency of thin (pouring) cream. As you continue to whisk, the volume should increase. After about 8–10 minutes, you will be able to see the bottom of the bowl, which means the mixture is cooked.

Tip the water out of the saucepan and drape a tea towel (dish towel) over the empty pan. Put the bowl back in the saucepan, resting on the tea towel to reduce movement and keep it nicely stabilised. Pour a thin stream of clarified butter into the egg mixture, building the sauce by whisking constantly as you would a mayonnaise until all the butter has been incorporated. Stir in the fresh mint and lemon juice and season to taste with salt and pepper. Set aside until required.

Heat a large frying pan or chargrill pan over very high heat and drizzle over the olive oil. Add the lamb cutlets (in batches if necessary) and cook for 2 minutes on each side, or until nicely caramelised and cooked to your liking. Transfer to a plate, cover with foil and leave to rest for a few minutes.

Garnish the cutlets with mint leaves and serve with the mint hollandaise and a side of your favourite vegetables.

Stuffed MUSSELS PROVENÇALE

2 tablespoons olive oil

100 g (3½ oz) speck bacon, cut into lardons

2 brown onions, finely chopped

4 garlic cloves, finely chopped

500 ml (17 fl oz/2 cups) tomato passata (puréed tomatoes)

15 g (½ oz/¼ cup) panko breadcrumbs

handful of parsley leaves

handful of basil leaves

8–10 thyme sprigs, leaves picked

handful of chives, coarsely chopped

pinch of freshly grated nutmeg

400 g (14 oz) chunky pork and fennel sausages, skin removed

2 eggs

sea salt and freshly ground black pepper

2 kg (4 lb 8 oz) black mussels, cleaned and debearded

250 ml (9 fl oz/1 cup) dry white wine

crusty bread, to serve

I suppose this is the French version of a 'surf & turf'! It my be a bit fiddly to prepare and eat but the combination of plump sweet mussels and pork mince cooked together in a rich tomato sauce is quite delicious. A good chunk of bread is a must to finish off the wonderful juices.

Put a large saucepan or stockpot over medium–high heat and drizzle in the olive oil. When hot, add the speck and half the onion and cook for 5–6 minutes, stirring occasionally, until lightly golden. Add half the garlic and cook for 1 minute. Pour in the tomato passata, bring to the boil and cook for a further 2 minutes. Set aside.

Put the breadcrumbs, herbs, nutmeg and remaining onion and garlic in a large bowl and mix until just combined. Add the sausage meat and eggs and mix to combine. Season to taste with salt and pepper.

Preheat the oven to 220°C (425°F).

Put the mussels in a large saucepan or stockpot, pour over the wine and cover with a lid. Bring to the boil over high heat and cook for 2 minutes only – you just want to open the mussels and make sure they are not overcooked. Drain the mussels, reserving the liquid and adding it to the tomato sauce, then set aside to cool. Discard any mussels that have not opened.

Using a teaspoon, fill the open shells of each mussel with some of the pork mixture and secure each one with kitchen string, looping the mussel three or four times.

Arrange the mussels side by side in an ovenproof dish, pour over the tomato sauce and bake for 18–20 minutes.

To serve, cut the string off the mussels and arrange them in a large bowl with the tomato sauce. Serve with plenty of crusty bread to dip into the sauce.

Steamed BLACK BEAN and PEPPER PORK RIBS

SERVES 4–6

1 kg (2 lb 4 oz) pork spare ribs, cut into bite-sized pieces

2 tablespoons peanut oil

1 x 4 cm (1½ inch) piece ginger, thinly sliced

2 garlic cloves, chopped

1 fresh long red chilli, thinly sliced

3 spring onions (scallions), sliced on the diagonal, whites and greens separated

steamed rice, to serve

MARINADE

2 teaspoons Chinese rice wine

1 tablespoon light soy sauce

1 teaspoon karamel masakan

2 teaspoons sesame oil

2 teaspoons sugar

1 teaspoon sea salt

½ teaspoon freshly ground black pepper

1 tablespoon cornflour (cornstarch)

1 tablespoon fermented black beans, soaked in water for 5 minutes, drained and coarsely chopped

Easy to make and totally delicious, this is Clarissa's version of a typical yum cha dish that most people really enjoy. If you can't get your hands on fermented black beans, you can use the same quantity of jarred black bean sauce, which is available in most supermarkets and Asian grocery stores these days.

To make the marinade, combine all the ingredients in a large bowl. Add the pork ribs and toss to coat, then cover and leave to marinate for at least 1 hour.

Heat the peanut oil in a large wok heat over medium–low heat, add the ginger and stir-fry for 2–3 minutes, or until lightly golden. Add the garlic and fry for 30 seconds.

Increase the heat to high, drain the pork from the marinade (reserving the marinade) and add to the wok. Cook for 5–6 minutes, stirring occasionally, until slightly caramelised. Add the chilli, reserved marinade and white spring onion and stir-fry for 1 minute, or until the liquid comes to the boil.

Transfer the pork stir-fry to a deep heatproof dish that fits snugly in a bamboo steamer, ensuring the dish has enough extra space for the sauce to expand as the steam trickles into it.

Bring water to the boil in a saucepan or a wok over high heat. Place the dish with pork ribs on a steaming rack. Cover and reduce the heat to low, then steam for 50 minutes, checking periodically to see if the ribs are soft and adding more water to the pan or wok, if necessary.

Once the ribs are tender, take the dish out and garnish with the green spring onion. Serve with steamed rice.

Basque Albacore TUNA STEW

SERVES 4

60 ml (2 fl oz/¼ cup) olive oil

1 red onion, finely diced

1 red capsicum (pepper), seeds removed, diced

1 green capsicum (pepper), seeds removed, diced

2 garlic cloves, finely chopped

1 fresh jalapeño chilli, seeded and finely chopped

½ teaspoon chilli flakes

sea salt

1 x 400 g (14 oz) tin chopped tomatoes

500 g roasting potatoes (e.g. russet [idaho] or king edward), cut into 2 cm (¾ inch) cubes

750 ml (26 fl oz/3 cups) Fish stock (see page 198) or water

600 g tuna or albacore steak, cut into 3 cm (1¼ inch) cubes

2 tablespoons finely chopped parsley

There are many recipes for fish stew from all around the globe but this one comes from the Basque country, a little place nestled between France and Spain. I use albacore here as it is a cheaper variety of tuna but still very tasty in a soup or stew preparation. This dish is best made on the day you want to serve it.

Heat 2 tablespoons of olive oil in a large heavy-based saucepan or enamelled cast-iron casserole dish over medium-high heat. Reduce the heat to medium, add the onion, capsicum, garlic, chilli, chilli flakes and a good pinch of salt and cook for 10–12 minutes, stirring occasionally, until the vegetables are very soft but not browning. Stir in the chopped tomatoes and potato.

Pour over the stock and bring to the boil, then reduce the heat to medium–low and simmer for 15–20 minutes, or until the potato is tender (but still has a bite) and the broth has thickened. Taste and add more salt if necessary.

Heat the remaining oil in a large frying pan over high heat. Season the tuna with salt and sear it in batches for 2–3 minutes until browned on at least two sides. Transfer to a plate and set aside.

Add the tuna to the stew and stir in 1 tablespoon of parsley. Remove from the heat and set aside for 3 minutes, or until the tuna is heated through but just barely cooked.

Spoon the stew into four warm bowls and garnish with the remaining parsley.

Three-spice ROAST PORK

4 roasting potatoes
(e.g. king edward),
cut into quarters

1 tablespoon coarsely
ground black pepper

1 kg (2 lb 4 oz) pork
belly, skin on

2 tablespoons karamel
masakan

1½ tablespoons sea salt

1 tablespoon sugar

160 ml (5¼ fl oz/⅔ cup)
vegetable oil

330 ml (11¼ fl oz) beer

2 teaspoons cornflour
(cornstarch) blended
with 1 tablespoon water

SPICE RUB

4 cinnamon sticks

8–10 cloves

8 star anise, ground

SAUCE

2 tablespoons caster
(superfine) sugar

2 teaspoons sea salt

2 tablespoons white vinegar

1 teaspoon karamel
masakan

1 teaspoon freshly ground
black pepper

This dish is unique to Clarissa's family. I know it seems unusual to call a recipe 'roast pork' only to coat it in spices and fry it, but this is now how we do it. And let me tell you, it's one of the most delicious, most fragrant 'roast' pork dinners you will ever try.

Put the potato in a saucepan of salted water over high heat and bring to the boil, then reduce the heat and simmer for 7–8 minutes (you just want to parboil them at this stage). Drain and place on a plate, uncovered, in the fridge for at least 30 minutes to dry out.

For the spice rub, toast the spices in a dry frying pan over medium heat for about 2 minutes, or until fragrant. Transfer to a spice grinder or mortar and pestle and grind to a fine powder.

Combine 1 tablespoon of the spice mix with the pepper (reserve any leftovers for your next family roast!) and rub over the pork flesh and skin. Mix together the karamel masakan, salt and sugar then, using wet hands, massage the paste into the spice-coated pork – the mixture is very thick but it will loosen up as you work it in. Place in a glass or ceramic dish, then cover and leave to marinate for 1 hour. For a more intense flavour, score the pork skin and rub in the marinade.

Heat the oil in a large wok over medium heat. Place the pork, skin side down, in the hot oil and shallow-fry for 15 minutes, carefully flipping over every 3–5 minutes to ensure the pork doesn't burn.

Push the pork to one side and add the potato to the wok, turning to coat in the oil. Continue to cook for another 15 minutes, turning the pork and potato every 3–5 minutes. Remove the potato from the wok – it should be dark golden on the outside and fork-tender on the inside. Cover and keep warm.

Remove the pork from the wok and drain the oil into a heatproof container. Return 80 ml (2½ fl oz/⅓ cup) of the oil to the wok, along with the pork. Carefully pour the beer around the pork and cook for another 20 minutes, turning the pork every 5 minutes this time. Remove the pork, place on a serving dish and cover with foil. Set aside to rest.

Add the sauce ingredients and 125 ml (4 fl oz/½ cup) of water to the wok and simmer for 10–15 minutes, or until reduced by half. Add the cornflour paste and whisk constantly for 1–2 minutes, or until the sauce is thick and glossy.

To serve, cut the pork into 1 cm (½ inch) thick slices. Arrange the potato around the pork and pour the sauce over the top.

THE CLASSIC SKATE WING *with* BROWN BUTTER SAUCE

SERVES 4

4 x 250 g (9 oz) skate wing pieces, skin removed (ask your fishmonger to do this for you)

1 carrot, thinly sliced

1 small brown onion, thinly sliced

2 bay leaves

12 black peppercorns

60 ml (2 fl oz/¼ cup) olive oil

120 g (4¼ oz) butter

80 ml (2½ fl oz/⅓ cup) red wine vinegar

1–2 tablespoons capers, rinsed

small handful of parsley leaves

steamed asparagus and green beans, to serve

It may surprise you to hear that this is one of the oldest recipes in the French culinary repertoire. Skate is an underused fish here in Australia, but I urge you to try this wonderful dish; the delicate flesh covered with capers and lashes of slightly burnt butter is a marriage made in heaven.

Place the skate wings in a large deep frying pan and pour in enough water to cover. Add the carrot, onion, bay leaves and peppercorns, then place over medium–high heat and bring to the boil. Immediately reduce to a simmer and let the skate bubble very gently for 10–15 minutes, or until it is opaque and tender. Carefully lift the fish from the cooking liquid, place it on a dish and set aside. Discard the liquid.

Drizzle the olive oil into a large non-stick frying pan and place over medium–high heat. When very hot, fry the wing pieces for couple of minutes on each side until caramelised. Remove and put them on a warm plate.

Melt the butter in the same frying pan and watch it carefully as it begins to foam. As soon as it turns a pale nut brown (be quick as it will go black in seconds), pour in the vinegar and add the capers and parsley. Immediately pour the butter sauce over the fish and serve with steamed asparagus and green beans (or other vegetables of your choice).

Alsatian BACON and ONION TARTS

SERVES 4

125 g (4½ oz) crème fraîche

250 g (9 oz) quark

sea salt and freshly ground black pepper

240 g (8½ oz) plain (all-purpose) flour, plus extra for dusting

1 teaspoon baking powder

2 egg yolks

100 ml (3½ fl oz) olive oil

10 smoked bacon or speck bacon rashers, thinly sliced

1 large white onion, thinly sliced

NO! It's not a pizza, it's a very traditional recipe from Alsace, on the border between France and Germany. If you want to make it a bit fancier you can always add mushrooms or grated gruyère cheese or a washed-rind cheese like Reblochon – or if you are a 'gourmand' pig like me, all of the above.

Combine the crème fraîche, quark and salt and pepper in a bowl. Set aside.

Whisk the flour, baking powder and 1 teaspoon of salt in a bowl. Make a well in the centre.

Whisk together the egg yolks, 60 ml (2 fl oz/¼ cup) of olive oil and 125 ml (4 fl oz/½ cup) of water in a bowl or jug, and pour into the well. Using a fork, stir until a loose dough forms. Turn out onto a lightly floured surface and knead the dough for 1 minute, then shape it into a disc, wrap it in plastic wrap and chill for about 30 minutes; this will make it easier to roll out.

Preheat the oven to 250°C (500°F). If you have one, place a pizza stone on the centre rack; otherwise use a thick baking tray.

Place a frying pan over medium heat and drizzle in the remaining olive oil. When hot, add the bacon and cook for about 5 minutes, or until caramelised. Remove to a plate. Add the onion to the same pan, reduce the heat to low and cook slowly for 8–10 minutes, or until translucent but without colour. Set aside.

Divide the dough into four pieces. Working with one piece at a time, roll it out to a 23 cm (9 inch) round and place on a sheet of baking paper. Spread a quarter of the cheese mixture over the top, leaving a 1 cm (½ inch) border around the edge. Sprinkle with a quarter of the bacon and onion mixture. Transfer the dough (on the baking paper) to the pizza stone or baking tray. (If you like, you can bake two tarts at a time without affecting the cooking time.)

Reduce the oven temperature to 220°C (425°F) and bake for 8–10 minutes, or until lightly browned and crispy. Repeat with the remaining tarts. Enjoy! (I have no doubt you will.)

TROUT *wrapped* in PROSCIUTTO

12 thin slices prosciutto

100 g (3½ oz) butter

1 brown onion,
finely chopped

100 g (3½ oz) panko
breadcrumbs

2 tablespoons finely
chopped parsley

2 tablespoons finely
chopped sage

sea salt and freshly ground
black pepper

4 x 350 g (12 oz) whole
rainbow trout, cleaned
and scaled

juice of 1 lemon

watercress salad,
to serve (optional)

I love trout – it's such a delicate freshwater fish. Combine it with a handful of well-chosen ingredients and it becomes the king of the river. If you don't want your house to be too smelly after cooking you have my permission to use the barbecue. It might actually bring some smokiness to the prosciutto.

Preheat the oven to 200°C (400°F) and line a baking tray with baking paper.

Julienne four slices of prosciutto and reserve the rest to wrap the fish.

Place a large frying pan over medium heat, add half the butter and fry the julienned prosciutto for 1–2 minutes, or until beginning to crisp. Add the onion and cook slowly for about 5 minutes, or until just soft – reduce the heat if the onion starts to catch. Add the breadcrumbs and cook until lightly golden. Transfer the mixture to a heatproof bowl and leave to cool slightly, then add the parsley and sage and season to taste with salt and pepper.

Stuff each trout with one-quarter of the breadcrumb mixture and wrap each fish with two slices of prosciutto.

Arrange the trout on the prepared tray and top with knobs of the remaining butter and a good grinding of pepper. Bake for 20–25 minutes, or until the prosciutto is nice and crispy and the fish is flaking away from the bone.

Finish with a squeeze of lemon juice and serve with a watercress salad, if desired.

Braised BEEF CHEEKS with BLACK OLIVES

2 kg (4 lb 8 oz) beef cheeks

5 garlic cloves, peeled
and left whole

2 brown onions, thinly sliced

4 carrots, cut into 2 cm
(¾ inch) thick rounds

1 x 750 ml (26 fl oz) bottle of
red wine (preferably cabernet
sauvignon or shiraz)

60 ml (2 fl oz/¼ cup) olive oil

sea salt and freshly ground
black pepper

2 tablespoons plain
(all-purpose) flour

6 thyme sprigs,
plus extra to garnish

3 fresh bay leaves

8 black peppercorns

500 ml (17 fl oz/2 cups)
Beef stock (see page 198)

250 g (9 oz) black olives
(preferably sun-dried)

Another rich and beautiful beef stew, this time from the inland area of the south-west of France, where you will find wild red rice as well as wild bulls trained by French cowboys! It's a gorgeous part of the country.

Put the beef cheeks, garlic, onion and carrot in a glass or ceramic bowl. Pour over the red wine and cover with plastic wrap. Marinate in the fridge overnight or for a minimum of 12 hours.

The next day, drain the marinade and reserve. Place the beef on paper towel and pat dry. Reserve the vegetables.

Put a large, deep, heavy-based saucepan or flameproof casserole dish over medium–high heat. When hot, drizzle in 1½ tablespoons of olive oil. Season the beef with salt and pepper, then add to the hot pan in batches and brown for 3 minutes, or until caramelised all over, stirring occasionally. Return all the browned beef to the pan, add the reserved vegetables and cook for 5 minutes, or until nicely caramelised.

Stir in the flour and add the thyme, bay leaves and peppercorns, then pour the stock and reserved marinade over the beef. Cover and bring to the boil over high heat. Reduce the heat to medium–low and simmer gently for 1–1½ hours. Add the olives and cook for another 1–1½ hours, or until the beef is very tender. Season to taste with salt and pepper.

Garnish with extra thyme sprigs and serve with your favourite potato dish (such as Cheesy mashed potato, page 140), polenta or even pasta.

SQUID STEW *in* INK

2 ripe tomatoes

60 ml (2 fl oz/¼ cup) olive oil

2 leeks, pale part only, coarsely chopped

4 white onions, coarsely chopped

1 garlic clove, coarsely chopped

1 kg (2 lb 4 oz) squid tubes and tentacles, cleaned

2 tablespoons squid ink

60 ml (2 fl oz/¼ cup) Fish stock (see page 198) or water, plus extra if needed

Once when I was visiting the Basque country I was invited to go hand-line squid fishing by some local fishermen. We caught some beautiful fresh squid, but the best part of the day was when they cooked this stew, which we enjoyed together with a glass or two of red wine. It was great, and now I'd like to share their recipe with you.

Squid ink can be purchased in a jar from your fishmonger or a good deli.

Cut a shallow cross in the base of each tomato, plunge into a small saucepan of boiling water for 60 seconds, then transfer immediately to a bowl of iced water. Peel off the skins and coarsely chop the flesh.

Put a deep frying pan over medium heat and pour in the olive oil. When smoking, add the leek, onion and garlic and cook, stirring occasionally, for 8–10 minutes, or until soft and slightly golden.

Place the squid tubes and tentacles in a single layer on top of the vegetables and cook on each side for 5 minutes.

Lift out the squid, tipping any liquid inside the tubes back into the pan, and place in a bowl. Stir the squid ink into the vegetables and cook gently over low heat for 5 minutes, then transfer the mixture to a food processor or blender. Pour in the stock or water and blend until smooth, adding a little more liquid if the sauce is too thick.

Return the squid to the pan and pour over the sauce. Cover and cook over medium–low heat for another 10 minutes, or until the squid is tender and the sauce has thickened. Serve immediately.

My SALMON WELLINGTON

400 g (14 oz) flat cap or
swiss brown mushrooms,
coarsely chopped

3 golden shallots,
coarsely chopped

3 garlic cloves, crushed

½ teaspoon lemon thyme leaves

60 ml (2 fl oz/¼ cup) olive oil

30 g (1 oz) butter, plus 100 g
(3½ oz) extra, melted

1–2 tablespoons white wine

sea salt and freshly ground
black pepper

iced water

1 large leek

8 round sheets of brik pastry

1 side of salmon
(about 800 g/1 lb 12 oz),
centre cut, skin removed
and pin-boned

Buerre blanc sauce
(see page 202) and steamed
green vegetables, to serve

I have a soft spot for this lovely recipe. It came to me one day when I'd invited a group of friends over for dinner. I was planning to serve beef wellington – until I was told that one of my guests didn't eat meat. I didn't want to change my menu so I decided to tackle wellington in a different way. I'm happy to say it was very well received by all, and is something I've enjoyed making many times since then.

Preheat the oven to 230°C (450°F) and line a baking tray with baking paper.

Put the mushroom, shallot, garlic and lemon thyme in a food processor and pulse until finely chopped.

Combine the olive oil and butter in a large frying pan over medium heat. Add the mushroom mixture and cook for 8–10 minutes, or until most of the liquid has evaporated. Pour in the wine and cook for a further 5–7 minutes, or until evaporated. Season to taste with salt and pepper and set aside to cool.

Bring a saucepan of salted water to the boil over high heat. Have ready a large bowl of iced water.

Cut off the top dark-green part of the leek and discard. Cut the leek in half lengthways and wash well under a cold tap, then plunge into the boiling water for 1 minute, or until soft. Remove immediately and place in the iced water to stop the cooking process. Remove the leek ribbons and pat dry on a tea towel (dish towel) to remove all the excess water. Set aside.

Place four sheets of brik pastry on your work surface so one-quarter of each is overlapping to make one large square-ish sheet. Brush with melted butter, then place the remaining sheets on top in the same way. Brush again with melted butter.

In the centre of the pastry sheet, arrange the leek ribbons side by side in slightly overlapping rows to the same length as the salmon fillet.

Using a palette knife, spread the mushroom paste over the leek ribbons, then place the salmon fillet on top and season with salt and pepper. Fold the shorter edges of the brick pastry over the salmon. Take one side of the pastry and, keeping it nice and tight, roll the pastry, leek and mushroom paste around the salmon to form a tight barrel shape. Brush the other end of the pastry with butter to seal.

Transfer the wellington to the prepared baking tray, seam side down, and brush all over with the remaining melted butter. Bake for 10–12 minutes, or until the pastry is golden and crisp. Allow to rest for 6–8 minutes before slicing.

Serve with beurre blanc sauce and your favourite steamed greens.

BRAISED PORK BELLY *in* SOY *with* HARD-BOILED EGGS

SERVES 4

1 kg (2 lb 4 oz) pork belly, cut into 4 cm (1½ inch) cubes

4 large eggs

60 ml (2 fl oz/¼ cup) vegetable oil

1 garlic bulb, skin on and lightly bruised

1 cinnamon stick

1 star anise

4 cloves

100 g (3½ oz) fried tofu puffs (optional)

steamed rice, to serve

MARINADE

1 tablespoon karamel masakan

½ teaspoon Chinese five-spice powder

60 ml (2 fl oz/¼ cup) light soy sauce

1 tablespoon oyster sauce

1 teaspoon freshly ground white pepper

1 teaspoon sea salt

2 tablespoons sugar

SEASONING

1 teaspoon karamel masakan

2 tablespoons light soy sauce

1 tablespoon sugar

sea salt, to taste

Flavoursome and hearty, this Malaysian favourite is comfort food at its best. It's a dish with many variations, and some people ditch the spices altogether and simply flavour it with soy sauce. Clarissa likes the depth that the spices bring so this is the way we have it at home.

To make the marinade, combine all the ingredients in a large bowl. Add the pork and turn to coat well, then cover and marinate for 30 minutes.

Bring a medium saucepan of water to the boil and carefully add the eggs. Reduce the heat to medium and simmer for 9 minutes, then cool the eggs under cold running water and remove the shells. Set aside.

Heat the oil in a clay pot or large heavy-based saucepan over medium–high heat and sear the pork for 3–5 minutes, or until lightly caramelised.

Add the garlic bulb, cinnamon stick, star anise and cloves and give it a good stir. Pour in 500 ml (17 fl oz/2 cups) of water and bring to the boil, then reduce the heat to medium–low and cook, covered, for 5 minutes. Pour in another 500 ml (17 fl oz/2 cups) of water and cook for 45–60 minutes, or until the sauce has reduced and thickened slightly and the pork is tender. Add the hard-boiled eggs and tofu puffs (if using) and continue to simmer over the lowest heat for another 5 minutes.

Stir in the seasoning ingredients and a little extra water if the sauce is too thick for your liking. Serve with steamed rice.

BEEF *Rendang*

60 g (2¼ oz)
desiccated coconut

125 ml (4 fl oz/½ cup)
peanut oil

60 g (2¼ oz) tamarind pulp

60 ml (2 fl oz/¼ cup)
boiling water

1 lemongrass stem, bruised

1.5 kg (3 lb 5 oz) topside
or chuck steak, thickly sliced

8 kaffir lime leaves,
thinly sliced, plus extra
to garnish

50 g (1¾ oz/¼ cup)
coconut sugar,
plus extra if needed

1 tablespoon sea salt,
plus extra if needed

500 ml (17 fl oz/2 cups)
coconut cream

roti and/or steamed rice,
to serve

SPICE PASTE

10 dried long red chillies,
soaked in hot water for
30 minutes, drained

3 large red onions

6 garlic cloves

1 x 4 cm (1½ inch) piece ginger

1 x 4 cm (1½ inch) piece galangal

3 lemongrass stems,
pale part only

1 teaspoon ground coriander

1 teaspoon ground fennel

1 teaspoon ground cumin

1 teaspoon freshly ground
black pepper

1 teaspoon ground turmeric

There are many different versions of this classic dish, and I imagine each one incorporates a little something that was passed down by the cook's mother or grandmother. This recipe is one that Clarissa has made with her mother and aunt Julia a few times. Please be patient; it does take a long time to cook but it is most definitely worth the wait!

Tip the desiccated coconut into a dry frying pan or wok and gently toast over medium heat, stirring with a spatula to evenly disperse the heat, for 5–10 minutes, or until golden and toasty-smelling. Some bits may toast more slowly or quickly than others – don't worry as long as the general distribution is golden brown. Transfer the toasted coconut to a bowl and allow to cool, then pulse in a food processor for a minute or so until it resembles sawdust (or pound by hand with a mortar and pestle).

For the spice paste, coarsely chop the chillies, onions, garlic, ginger, galangal and lemongrass, place in a food processor with the spices and process to a fine paste. Add 1–2 tablespoons of water, if required, to help loosen it.

Heat the peanut oil in a large heavy-based saucepan or wok over medium–high heat until smoking. Add the spice paste, then reduce the heat to medium–low and stir-fry for 10–12 minutes, or until the oil separates. The paste will stick to the bottom, which is fine, but make sure you scrape it off as it cooks so it doesn't burn.

Mix the tamarind pulp with the boiling water, then press it through a fine sieve to make a paste.

Add the bruised lemongrass stem and beef to the pan or wok and stir-fry for 2 minutes, or until the beef is well coated in the paste. Add the kaffir lime leaf, tamarind paste, sugar, salt and 500 ml (17 fl oz/2 cups) of water and simmer over medium heat for 15 minutes.

Pour in the coconut cream, reduce the heat to low and simmer without a lid for 1½–2 hours, stirring occasionally. Add the toasted coconut and cook for another 30 minutes, or until the meat is really tender and the sauce has thickened.

Adjust the flavours with salt, tamarind and sugar if needed, garnish with extra kaffir lime and serve with roti and/or steamed rice.

Manu
126

Crumbed GARFISH and CRISPY CHIPS SERVES 4

3 eggs

2½ tablespoons cold water

sea salt and freshly ground black pepper

250 g (9 oz/1⅔ cups) plain (all-purpose) flour

250 g (9 oz) panko breadcrumbs

1 tablespoon coarsely chopped lemon thyme

200 g butter, melted

8 x 150 g garfish, butterflied (head and tails on for presentation)

lemon cheeks, to serve

CRISPY CHIPS

4 large or 6 medium all-purpose potatoes (e.g. coliban or sebago), washed

1½ tablespoons olive oil

2 garlic cloves, crushed

2 teaspoons sea salt

1 teaspoon freshly ground black pepper

I know you might wonder if we need another recipe for fish and chips, but trust me on this. I was introduced to garfish when I first arrived in Australia – it's a fabulous fish and perfect for frying or oven-baking. When you get your hands on this quiet achiever you'll understand. While garfish are available all year round, their peak season is March to May. Whiting would make a great substitute if garfish are unavailable.

Preheat the oven to 220°C (425°C) and line a baking tray with baking paper.

To make the chips, cut each potato into 2 cm (¾ inch) thick wedges and place in a large bowl. Drizzle with the olive oil and sprinkle over the garlic, salt and pepper. Toss well to coat, then arrange on the prepared tray and roast for 35–40 minutes, or until crisp and golden.

Meanwhile, crack the eggs into a shallow dish and whisk in the water and some salt and pepper.

Pour the flour into another shallow dish.

Put the breadcrumbs and lemon thyme in a shallow dish and season with pepper. Pour in half the melted butter and mix well - the idea is to coat all the breadcrumbs in butter so they turn golden in the oven.

Place a piece of baking paper on a baking tray and brush with some of the remaining butter.

Coat each fish in the flour, shaking off the excess, dip in the egg mixture and then press each side of the fish into the crumbs until well coated.

Place the garfish on the prepared tray, leaving a 2 cm (¾ inch) space between each fillet. Season well and drizzle with the remaining melted butter.

Bake the fish for 4–6 minutes, or until crisp and golden. Serve with crispy chips and lemon cheeks.

COCONUT *sambal-stuffed* FISH

SERVES 4

40 g (1½ oz/½ cup)
desiccated coconut

90 g (3¼ oz/⅓ cup) Sambal
belacan (see page 208)

60 ml (2 fl oz/¼ cup)
lime juice

2 tablespoons sugar

1 tablespoon sea salt,
plus extra for rubbing

4 x 250 g (9 oz) whole blue
mackerels, cleaned and scaled

vegetable oil, for deep-frying

steamed rice or Our fried rice
(see page 86), to serve

Sambal-stuffed fried fish is a popular dish in Malaysia when you have 'nasi campur', which literally means mixed rice. It's a stall that sells different dishes of meat, seafood, vegetables and condiments – you make your selection and they are served with rice. This recipe comes from Clarissa's mother.

Combine the desiccated coconut, sambal, lime juice, sugar and salt in a bowl and set aside for 30 minutes. Divide the mixture between two dishes – one to use for stuffing the fish and one to serve as a side.

Rinse the mackerels and pat dry. Cut a 1 cm (½ inch) deep pocket on either side of the backbone, from head to tail.

Rub the fish with a little extra salt, then stuff the sambal mixture into the pockets you have created. Put a teaspoon of the mixture in the cavity of each fish as well.

Pour the oil into a deep frying pan to a depth of 2 cm (¾ inch). Heat over medium-high heat until the oil reaches 180°C (350°C), or until a cube of bread dropped in the oil browns in 15 seconds. Carefully place the mackerel in the hot oil (in batches if necessary so you don't overcrowd the pan) and fry on one side for 2–3 minutes, then turn gently and fry on the other side for another 2–3 minutes. Remove from the pan and drain on paper towel. Keep warm until all the fish is cooked.

Serve with steamed or fried rice and the reserved sambal mixture.

FISH and TAMARIND CURRY

10 g (¼ oz) tamarind pulp

100 ml (3½ fl oz) boiling water

2 large red onions,
coarsely chopped

2 garlic cloves,
peeled and left whole

2 candlenuts

80 ml (2½ fl oz/⅓ cup)
sunflower oil

1 tablespoon chilli powder,
or to taste

¼ teaspoon ground aniseed

½ teaspoon ground turmeric

¼ teaspoon ground cumin

500 g (1 lb 2 oz) mackerel or
other firm-fleshed white fish,
skin removed and pin-boned,
cut into 4 cm (1½ inch) chunks

⅓–½ fresh pineapple,
peeled, cored and cut into
4 cm (1½ inch) cubes,
then halved lengthways

2 teaspoons sea salt

1½ tablespoons coconut
or soft brown sugar

2 teaspoons soy sauce

sliced fresh green chilli,
to garnish (optional)

steamed rice, to serve

If you have never tried this dish before, you must rectify that immediately. It's become one of my favourite meals and I'm always asking Clarissa to make it for me. I've even learnt to eat it the Malaysian way – with my fingers!

Soak the tamarind pulp in the boiling water for 15 minutes. When cooled, squeeze with your fingers to separate the tamarind flesh from the seeds. Pour the tamarind mixture into a sieve set over a bowl to catch the juice. Using your hand or a spoon, stir and press to extract as much tamarind juice as possible. Discard the fibres, membranes and seeds left in the sieve and set the juice aside.

Put the onion, garlic and candlenuts in a large mortar and pestle and pound to a thick coarse paste. (Alternatively, put them in a small food processor and process to a coarse paste.)

Heat a large deep frying pan over high heat and add the oil. Once smoking, reduce the heat to medium, add the onion paste and fry for 8–10 minutes, or until golden, then stir in the chilli, aniseed, turmeric and cumin. Continue frying until the paste becomes fragrant and caramelised – take care not to let it burn.

Add the reserved tamarind juice and bring the curry sauce to the boil. Add the fish and pineapple, then pour over about 300 ml (10½ fl oz) of water until the fish is covered. Stir in the salt, sugar and soy sauce. Bring to the boil, then reduce the heat to low and cook for 10 minutes, or until the sauce is thick and the fish is cooked through and flakes easily when gently pressed.

Before serving, taste for seasoning and add a little more sugar, salt and/or tamarind if necessary. Garnish with green chilli, if you like, and serve with steamed rice.

PORK CUTLETS *with a* WARM FENNEL *and* CAPSICUM JAM

SERVES 4

4 x 200 g (7 oz) pork cutlets

sea salt and freshly ground black pepper

olive oil, for pan-frying

2 garlic cloves, skin on, crushed

4 thyme sprigs, plus extra to garnish (optional)

60 g (2¼ oz) butter

FENNEL AND CAPSICUM JAM

60 ml (2 fl oz/¼ cup) extra virgin olive oil

1 small or ½ fennel bulb, tough outer layer discarded, thinly sliced

1 brown onion, thinly sliced

1 red capsicum (pepper), seeds removed, thinly sliced

sea salt and freshly ground black pepper

1 tablespoon caster (superfine) sugar

60 ml (2 fl oz/¼ cup) red wine vinegar

handful of sage leaves, shredded

I know what you're thinking: where's the sauce? Well relax! The caramelised fennel and capsicum jam does the job perfectly here. And if you're still hungry and fancy a late-night snack later on, the jam also goes very well with cheese and biscuits.

For the jam, heat 2 tablespoons of olive oil in a large frying pan over medium heat. When hot, add the fennel, onion and capsicum. Season with salt and pepper to taste and add the sugar, then sauté for 5 minutes, or until soft and golden. Add the vinegar and let it bubble for 1–2 minutes. Reduce the heat to low, add the remaining olive oil and cook for 20–25 minutes, or until the onion is well caramelised and jammy. Stir in the shredded sage and cook for 30 seconds, then remove from the heat. Transfer to a bowl and set aside to infuse.

Wipe the pan clean, ready to cook the pork.

Using a sharp knife, make incisions into the fat of the cutlets, about 5 mm (¼ inch) deep and at 2 cm (¾ inch) intervals, making sure you don't cut into the meat. Season the cutlets well on both sides.

Place the frying pan over high heat and, when hot, and add a dash of olive oil. Add the cutlets, garlic and thyme and fry for 2–3 minutes, or until coloured. Turn and fry for a further 2–3 minutes on the other side, pushing the thyme under the pork and breaking up the garlic a little. Towards the end of the cooking time, add the butter and baste the cutlets with it. Transfer the cutlets to a plate and rest for 5 minutes, spooning over all the pan juices.

To serve, place spoonfuls of jam on warm serving plates, top each with a cutlet and finish with a drizzle of the resting juices. Garnish with extra thyme sprigs, if you like.

Hainanese CHICKEN RICE

SERVES 4–6

While Clarissa's mother is of Peranakan descent, her great grandfather came from the Hainan province in China, so the family is (happily) obliged to make the great Hainanese chicken rice. This silky-smooth chicken is the epitome of what braised chicken should taste like. I know the recipe seems a little daunting as it does have a lot of steps, but it's only scary the first time, right? My suggestion is to read the recipe a couple of times before you start – get your head around the processes and you'll be fine!

1 x 1.6 kg (3 lb 8 oz) chicken (preferably organic or free-range)

140 g (5 oz/½ cup) fine sea salt

200 g (7 oz) sliced ginger, skin on

2 spring onions (scallions), halved

iced water, to cover

1 tablespoon sesame oil

CHICKEN RICE

500 g (1 lb 2 oz) chicken skin or 80 g (2¾ oz) butter

3 garlic cloves, finely chopped

2 red Asian shallots, finely chopped

1 x 4 cm (1½ inch) piece ginger, finely chopped

400 g (14 oz/2 cups) long-grain or jasmine rice, rinsed and drained

1 teaspoon sea salt

1.25 litres (44 fl oz/5 cups) reserved chicken poaching broth

½ teaspoon sesame oil

CHILLI SAUCE

1 tablespoon lime juice

2 tablespoon reserved chicken poaching broth, skimmed from the top of the broth to catch the extra fat

2 teaspoons sugar

8 fresh long red chillies

3 garlic cloves

1 x 3 cm (1¼ inch) piece ginger

½ teaspoon sea salt, or to taste

GINGER AND SPRING ONION SAUCE

1 x 6 cm (2½ inch) piece ginger, finely chopped

3 spring onions (scallions), thinly sliced

sea salt, to taste

60 ml (2 fl oz/¼ cup) peanut oil

GRAVY FOR CHICKEN

1 teaspoon oyster sauce

1 teaspoon soy sauce

80 ml (2½ fl oz/⅓ cup) reserved chicken poaching broth, skimmed from the top of the broth

1 teaspoon sesame oil

dash of freshly ground white pepper

SIDES AND GARNISH

crispy fried shallots

60 ml (2 fl oz/¼ cup) soy sauce

1 Lebanese cucumber, halved lengthways andthinly sliced

2 spring onions (scallions), thinly sliced on the diagonal

sliced fresh red chilli, to taste

4–6 coriander sprigs (optional)

Place the chicken on a chopping board. Start with a small handful of salt and rub it gently over the skin of the whole chicken, almost like you are exfoliating and massaging it. Take your time doing this, as it is to get rid of the trapped gunk and to give it a smoother skin. Rub for 15–20 minutes using more salt as required, then rinse and pat dry. You will find that the skin now glistens and is a little more taut. Season the inside and outside of the chicken with 1–2 tablespoons of salt, then stuff the ginger and halved spring onions into the cavity of the chicken.

Fill a large stockpot or saucepan with enough water to cover the chicken (about 5–6 litres/175–210 fl oz) and bring to the boil over high heat. Place the chicken in the pot, breast side down, and return to the boil. Once boiling, immediately reduce the heat to low and simmer very gently, uncovered, for 25–30 minutes, spooning off any scum from the surface as required. It is very important that you don't let the water boil rapidly and it should just cover the chicken. Remove the pan from the heat and let the chicken stand in the hot broth for 15–20 minutes, covered and undisturbed, until it is just cooked through.

While the chicken is standing in the broth, take a pan of a similar size or bigger than the one the chicken was cooked in and fill with iced water, using lots of ice as it needs to be icy cold.

As soon as the chicken is ready, gently lift it out of the broth using two plastic slotted spoons or spatulas. Do not attempt to lift it out with tongs, as you will tear the delicate skin on the chicken. You can check that it is cooked by inserting a skewer into the flesh between the leg and the breast – the juices should run clear. If you prefer to use a meat thermometer, it should read 80°C (170°F).

Lower the chicken into the iced water, discarding the ginger and spring onion from the cavity. Reserve the broth. Allow the chicken to cool completely, turning it once in the iced water. (Plunging the chicken into the iced water stops the cooking process immediately and tightens the skin, which is important. This dish is all about the texture of the skin!) When the chicken has cooled, drain it and pat dry with paper towel. Rub the outside of the chicken with sesame oil to prevent it from drying out.

Skim about 125 ml (4 fl oz/½ cup) of liquid and fat off the top layer of the broth and reserve for the chilli sauce and chicken gravy.

For the chicken rice, to render the fat from the skin, cook the chicken skin in a heavy-based saucepan over medium heat, stirring occasionally, until rendered, then discard the solids. This can be done ahead of time, transferred to a heatproof container and refrigerated until required. If you are using butter here you can leave this step out.

Place a large wok or frying pan over medium heat and add 80 g (2¾ oz) of the rendered chicken fat or butter. When hot, add the garlic, shallot and ginger and cook, stirring, for 2–3 minutes, or until golden. Add the rice and stir to combine. Cook for 3 minutes, then add the salt. Pour in the poaching broth and bring to the boil, then reduce the heat slightly but continue to boil for 3–4 minutes, or until the liquid on the surface has evaporated and small bubbles appear from the holes in the rice. Cover and cook over low heat for 15–18 minutes, or until the rice is tender and all the liquid has been absorbed.

(If you are using a rice cooker, put the cooked garlic and rice mixture in the cooker and add the broth. Cover and cook according to the manufacturer's instructions until the rice is tender and the liquid has been absorbed.)

Remove the pan from the heat and stand, covered and undisturbed, for 5 minutes. Fluff the rice with a fork, then drizzle with the sesame oil and fluff again. Cover and set aside until required.

To make the chilli sauce, put all the ingredients in a high-speed blender and process until smooth and bright red.

For the ginger and spring onion sauce, put the ginger, spring onion and salt in a heatproof dish. Heat the peanut oil until it is just starting to smoke, then pour over the ginger and spring onion mixture and stir to combine.

For the chicken gravy, combine all the ingredients in a medium bowl.

Before serving, bring any remaining poaching broth to the boil – this is to be served as soup on the side. Using a meat cleaver or carving scissors, cut the chicken in half down the breast bone and back bone, then separate the leg from the breast. Cut the four larger pieces into 3 cm (1¼ inch) slices. You should end up with about 20 pieces. Arrange on a large serving dish and pour the gravy over the chicken.

To serve, fill individual serving bowls with spoonfuls of chicken rice and sprinkle with crispy fried shallots. Ladle the hot broth into small side bowls, along with bowls of soy sauce, cucumber slices, ginger and spring onion sauce, and chilli sauce. Scatter spring onion, red chilli and coriander sprigs (if using) over the chicken and serve.

TIP:
Before you start cooking your chicken, it helps to prepare the ingredients for your sauces and rice. These are usually assembled after the chicken is done because they require the chicken broth, but you can get started on washing and draining the rice and chopping the garlic and ginger before then.

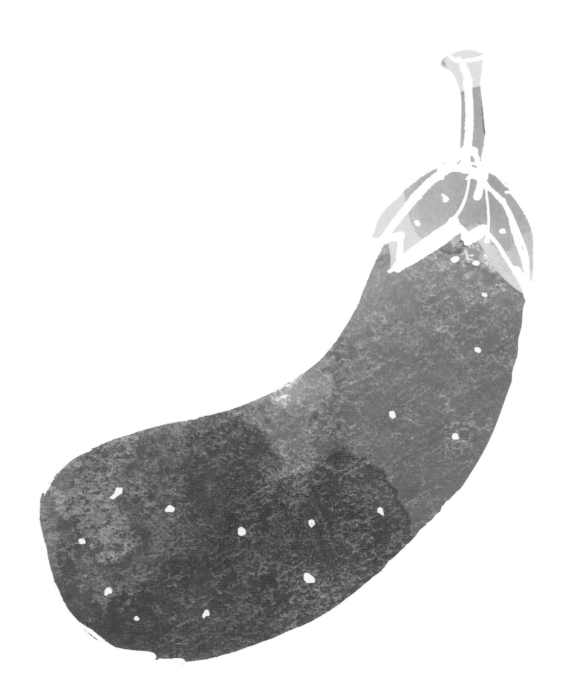

SIDES

I firmly believe that vegetables should be given the same respect and love we give to any other food. Much more than a simple dish on the side, they help set the tone of the meal, offering a contrasting kick of flavour or, in the case of my amazing mash, a comforting foil for rich meat dishes. In this chapter, we have included some classic recipes and a few surprises, just to keep things interesting.

Cheesy MASHED POTATO

1 kg (2 lb 4 oz) all-purpose potatoes (such as desiree or sebago)

200 g (7 oz) crème fraîche or sour cream

3 garlic cloves, crushed

500 g (1 lb 2 oz) strong cheddar cheese, grated

sea salt and freshly ground black pepper

I admit that pairing cheese and potato in one recipe sounds rather indulgent, but even those watching their calorie intake will want to make the occasional exception for this fabulous purée from the Pyrénées: pommes aligot. This dish traditionally uses Tomme de Laguiole or Tomme d'Auvergne cheese, but you can substitute these with a cantal or gruyère. If you find it difficult to source the more traditional cheeses or substitutes, don't give up! A cheese with a strong nutty flavour will do just as well – try a vintage cheddar with a little bit of mozzarella to give you the stringiness.

Peel the potatoes and cut them into large chunks. Put them in a large saucepan or stockpot, cover with cold salted water and bring to the boil over high heat. Reduce the heat to medium and cook at a strong simmer for 9–10 minutes, or until tender.

Drain well in a large sieve or colander. Push the potato through a potato ricer or fine sieve into the saucepan, then place over low heat. Stir in the crème fraîche or sour cream and garlic. Gradually add the cheese, a handful at a time, stirring with a wooden spoon as you go. The potato should become very stringy. Once all the cheese has been incorporated, season with salt and pepper to taste and serve immediately.

Grandma Marigold's
SRI LANKAN SPICY EGGPLANT

SERVES 4

1 tablespoon black
mustard seeds

1 x 4 cm (1½ inch) piece
ginger, coarsely chopped

2 garlic cloves, peeled
and left whole

250 ml (9 fl oz/1 cup)
vegetable oil

8 Japanese eggplants
(aubergines), cut lengthways
into quarters

5 red Asian shallots,
thinly sliced

2 curry leaf sprigs

1–2 teaspoons chilli powder

2 tablespoons white vinegar

2 teaspoons sea salt, or to taste

2 teaspoons sugar

Clarissa's grandparents on her father's side are of Sinhalese descent so she has been exposed to many wonderful Sri Lankan dishes. Her mother learnt this particular dish from her paternal grandmother, with whom they lived for most of Clarissa's early childhood. It's quite oily so it keeps for a week in the fridge.

Curry leaves add an authentic fragrance to this dish, and are available fresh, frozen or dried at Asian grocery stores and larger supermarkets.

Using a mortar and pestle, pound the mustard seeds, ginger and garlic to a paste and set aside.

Heat a large frying pan over low heat and pour in 60 ml (2 fl oz/¼ cup) of the oil. Add a single layer of eggplant wedges and fry for 8 minutes, turning after 4–5 minutes or once dark brown and charred. The eggplant will instantly absorb all the oil but will release it back into the pan as it cooks.

Continue cooking until the eggplant is tender, then remove it from the pan and drain well on paper towel. Add another tablespoon or two of oil to what is left in the pan and add another layer of eggplant. Repeat until all the eggplant has been fried and drained.

Top up (or remove) oil so you have 2 tablespoons in the pan and increase the heat to medium. Add the shallot and curry leaves and sauté for 3–4 minutes, or until soft and caramelised. Add the chilli powder and the mustard seed paste and fry for 1–2 minutes, or until fragrant. Add the vinegar, salt, sugar and 60 ml (2 fl oz/¼ cup) of water and mix well. Return the fried eggplant to the pan and toss to coat.

Serve hot or at room temperature.

MORE PLEASE!

PINEAPPLE *and* CUCUMBER SALAD

1 golden pineapple

2 Lebanese (short) cucumbers

80 ml (2½ fl oz/⅓ cup) white wine vinegar or apple cider vinegar

2 tablespoons sugar

½ teaspoon sea salt

1 fresh bird's eye chilli, thinly sliced (optional)

handful of coriander (cilantro) leaves, coarsely chopped, plus extra sprigs to garnish (optional)

Less of a salad and more of a palate cleanser, you can serve this with almost any curry or rich dish. The trick here is to achieve a nice balance of salty, sweet and sour, with a hint of chilli, if desired.

Cut off a generous slice from the top and bottom of the pineapple. Stand the pineapple upright, then work your way around, carefully cutting off the skin. Like the top and the bottom, the core can be very woody, so it's best to remove it. Cut the rest of the pineapple (the sweetest and juiciest part) into rough 1 cm (½ inch) dice.

Peel the skin off the cucumbers and cut them in half lengthways. Scoop out the seeds with a teaspoon or cut them out with a small, sharp knife. Cut the remaining flesh into cubes a similar size to the pineapple.

Put the pineapple, cucumber, vinegar, sugar and salt in a medium bowl, add the chilli and coriander (if using) and mix well with your hands. Taste to make sure you have a balance of sweet, sour and salty and adjust the flavours if necessary.

Serve at room temperature, garnished with coriander sprigs, if you like. If you're making this ahead of time in warm weather, store it in the fridge until needed, then bring it back to room temperature to serve.

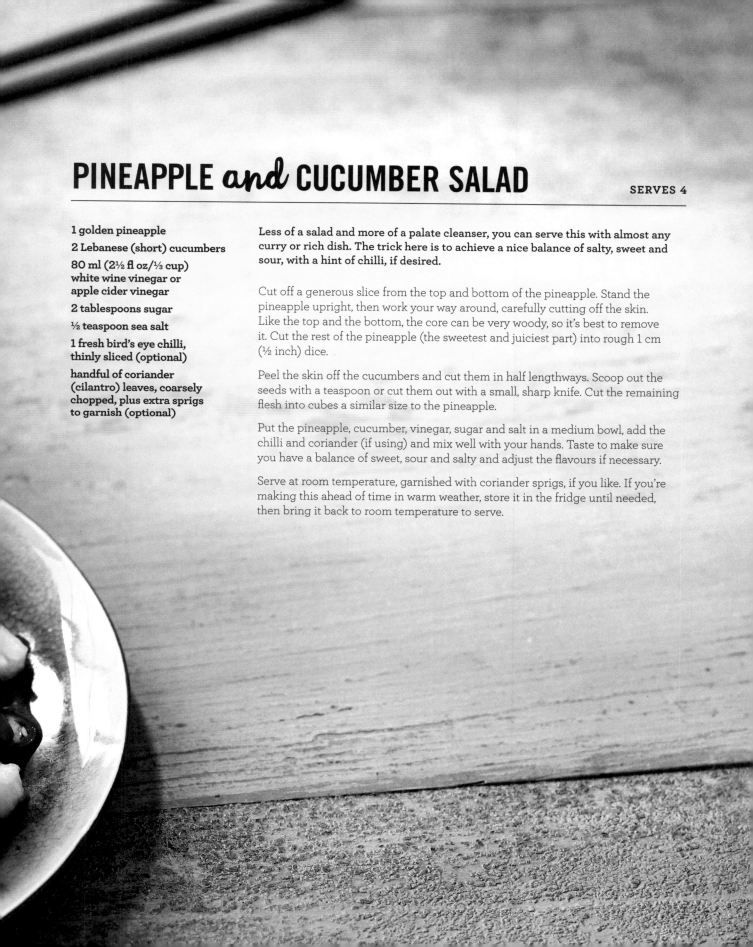

DUCK-FAT POTATOES *with* GARLIC *and* ROSEMARY

SERVES 6

6 large all-purpose potatoes (e.g. desiree or sebago)

160 g (5¾ oz/⅔ cup) duck fat, at room temperature

sea salt and freshly ground black pepper

4 garlic cloves, thinly sliced

16–18 thyme sprigs

8–10 young rosemary sprigs or sprig tips, cut into 5 cm (2 inch) lengths

Crisp golden potatoes are probably the one vegetable accompaniment that everyone loves – no matter what shape or form they come in. While the garlic and rosemary certainly add to the flavour of this dish, it is the duck fat that really makes it stand out. Just one taste and you'll be hooked.

Preheat the oven to 200°C (400°F) and line a baking tray with baking paper.

Scrub the potatoes under cold running water and pat dry. Put them on a chopping board, flattest side down, and cut horizontal slits into the potato, spacing them about 5 mm (¼ inch) apart. Take care not to cut all the way through – you want the slices to stay connected at the bottom of the potato.

Arrange the potatoes on the prepared tray. Brush all over with some of the duck fat, including the bottoms, and sprinkle generously with salt and pepper.

Bake for 30 minutes, or until the slices start separating. Brush the potatoes again with duck fat, making sure some of it drips down between the slices. Gently separate the slices, if necessary, and insert garlic slices and sprigs of thyme and rosemary in between.

Return the tray to the oven and bake for a further 30–35 minutes, or until the potatoes are crisp on the edges. Serve immediately, while the potatoes are at their crispest.

SQUID *Sambal*

1 large red onion,
coarsely chopped

2 garlic cloves,
coarsely chopped

125 ml (4 fl oz/½ cup)
vegetable oil

1 tablespoon Sambal belacan
(see page 208), or more to taste

500 g (1 lb 2 oz) squid tubes,
cleaned and cut into 1 cm
(½ inch) thick rings

1 tablespoon tamarind paste
or purée, or to taste

1 tablespoon sugar, or to taste

1 teaspoon sea salt, or to taste

2 teaspoons fish sauce,
or to taste

steamed rice or Coconut rice
(see page 92), to serve

I love this dish because it's hot and spicy! And if you have already cooked a batch of sambal belacan ahead of time, you can whip this up in minutes. It's great served simply with rice. If you would prefer to make a prawn sambal, simply replace the squid with the same weight of peeled and deveined raw prawns.

Put the red onion and garlic in a food processor or blender and pulse to a paste, adding 2–3 tablespoons of oil if needed to loosen the mixture.

Heat the remaining oil in a large wok or frying pan over medium–low heat, add the onion paste and sauté for 5–6 minutes, or until fragrant.

Stir in the sambal belacan, then add 60 ml (2 fl oz/¼ cup) of water and bring to a simmer. Add the squid and cook, turning occasionally, for 3–4 minutes, or until cooked through. Stir in the tamarind paste, sugar, salt and fish sauce, then taste and adjust the seasoning if necessary.

Serve with steamed rice or coconut rice.

MORE PLEASE!

Oven-baked RATATOUILLE

60 ml (2 fl oz/¼ cup)
olive oil

4 brown onions,
thinly sliced

4 garlic cloves,
thinly sliced

2 tablespoons thyme leaves

3 large zucchini (courgettes)

3 Japanese eggplants
(aubergines)

6 truss tomatoes

2 tablespoons coarsely
chopped rosemary

sea salt and freshly ground
black pepper

If you're not a big fan of vegetables, I have a feeling this recipe from the south of France will change your mind. Ripe vegetables are baked together with garlic and fresh herbs, and the result smells like summer.

Preheat the oven to 200°C (400°F).

Place a frying pan over medium heat, add 1 tablespoon of olive oil and sauté the onion for about 15 minutes, or until lightly golden, reducing the heat a little if the onion begins to catch. Add the garlic and 1 tablespoon of thyme and cook for 2 minutes. Spread the onion mixture over the base of a large roasting tin.

Wash the veggies and cut them widthways into 1 cm (½ inch) thick slices. Tightly arrange the vegetables in rows over the onion base, starting with the zucchini, followed by the eggplant then the tomato. Gently push the slices out so they sit in a diagonal pattern, exposing some of the flesh. Drizzle with the remaining olive oil and sprinkle over the rosemary and remaining thyme. Season with salt and pepper and bake for 45 minutes, or until the vegetables are tender.

MORE PLEASE!

SPICY POTATOES *with* DRIED PRAWNS

SERVES 4 AS A MAIN OR 6 AS A SIDE

30 g (1 oz) dried
prawns (shrimp)

boiling water, for soaking

160 ml (5¼ fl oz) vegetable oil

5 large roasting potatoes
(e.g. russet [idaho] or king
edward), cut into 1 cm
(½ inch) cubes

1 large red onion,
coarsely chopped

2 teaspoons Dried chilli
powder (see page 209),
or to taste

juice of 1 lime

2 teaspoons sugar

1 teaspoon soy sauce

1 teaspoon sea salt

Another scrumptious dish from Clarissa's childhood. Clarissa and I have
modified the method from her mum's original recipe, so that the potatoes
are sautéed until crisp on the outside and beautifully fluffy on the inside.
It tastes the same but better!

Put the dried prawns in a bowl, cover with boiling water and leave to soak
for 15 minutes to remove any excess salt. Drain well and coarsely chop.

Heat half the oil in a wok or large frying pan over medium–high heat, add
the potato and carefully stir to coat with the oil. Fry for 20–25 minutes, stirring
occasionally, until crisp and golden on all sides and soft in the centre. Tip into
a large bowl.

Return the pan to the heat, add the remaining oil and the onion and stir to coat.
Add the chopped dried prawns and fry for 5 minutes, or until the onion starts
to soften.

Add the chilli powder and sauté for another 2–3 minutes, then stir in the lime
juice, sugar, soy sauce and salt and mix well. Return the fried potato to the pan
and stir to coat with the prawn mixture. Adjust the seasoning if necessary, and
serve immediately.

Turmeric OKRA

500 g (1 lb 2 oz) okra

60 ml (2 fl oz/¼ cup) vegetable oil

2 teaspoons black mustard seeds

8 large red Asian shallots, thinly sliced

2 garlic cloves, thinly sliced

1 x 400 g (14 oz) tin coconut milk

2 sprigs curry leaves (or 20 dried leaves)

2 teaspoons ground turmeric

1 teaspoon sea salt, or to taste

1 teaspoon sugar

steamed rice, to serve (optional)

Clarissa grew up eating this simple but incredibly flavoursome dish. Every member of her family makes it, but they all have their own versions. This is beautiful with any curry dish, but we often just enjoy it on its own with rice.

Wash the okra and cut off the tops. Pat dry with paper towel.

Place a large wok over high heat and pour in the oil. When it is smoking, add the okra in small batches and stir-fry for 2–3 minutes. Remove with a slotted spoon or spider and drain on paper towel.

Add the mustard seeds and shallot to the wok and stir-fry over medium heat for 4–5 minutes, or until the shallot begins to caramelise. Add the garlic and stir-fry for 5 minutes, or until dark golden and lightly charred. Remove with a slotted spoon (to leave any excess oil in the wok). Be careful not to overcook this mixture as it will continue to cook after it is removed from the wok. Set aside until required.

Add the coconut milk, curry leaves and turmeric to the wok and bring to the boil. Immediately reduce the heat to low, then add the salt and sugar and simmer for 2–3 minutes, or until the sauce has thickened slightly. Add the okra to the sauce and simmer for 1 minute. Taste and adjust the seasoning, if necessary.

To serve, spoon the okra into a serving bowl and sprinkle over the caramelised onion, garlic and mustard seeds. Serve with steamed rice or as an accompaniment to a main meal.

Stir-fried SNAKE BEANS with DRIED PRAWNS

15 g (½ oz) dried prawns (shrimp)

boiling water, for soaking

80 ml (2½ fl oz/⅓ cup) vegetable oil

2 garlic cloves, thinly sliced

150 g (5½ oz) snake (long) beans, cut into 4 cm (1½ inch) lengths

½ teaspoon sea salt

1 teaspoon fish sauce

¼ teaspoon sugar

1–2 fresh bird's eye chillies, thinly sliced (optional)

steamed rice or Our fried rice (see page 86), to serve

This dish is essentially a 'jooshed' up version of a simple stir-fry using only garlic for flavouring. I love it with snake beans, but the beauty is that you can use this recipe for just about any type of vegetable. So get creative (but try it with beans first!).

Put the dried prawns in a bowl, cover with boiling water and leave to soak for 15 minutes to remove any excess salt. Drain well and coarsely chop.

Heat the oil in a wok or large frying pan over medium–high heat, add the chopped dried prawns and stir-fry for 1 minute. Add the garlic and stir-fry until it just becomes golden, being careful not to let it burn.

Add the beans and toss to combine, then cook for 5 minutes, or until the beans are tender and the mixture is dry. Add the salt, fish sauce, sugar and chilli (if using) and toss to combine.

Serve with steamed or fried rice.

Sambal WATER SPINACH

150 g (5½ oz) water spinach
or English spinach

2 tablespoons vegetable oil

2 garlic cloves,
thinly sliced

2 red Asian shallots,
thinly sliced

1 tablespoon Cooked sambal
chilli (see page 208)

1 teaspoon fish sauce

½ teaspoon sugar

sea salt

steamed rice,
to serve (optional)

Water spinach (also known as kangkung or ong choy) is like the Asian equivalent of English spinach, and its dark green leaves are packed with nutritional goodness. This humble dish is often served in Malaysian hawker stalls as an accompaniment to main dishes.

Pluck the spinach leaves from the stems and keep them whole. Chop the stems into 4 cm (1½ inch) lengths.

Heat the oil in a wok or large frying pan over medium-high heat. Add the garlic and shallot and stir-fry briskly. Add the sambal and cook for 30 seconds.

Add the spinach stems and toss to coat with the sambal mixture, then toss in the leaves and stir-fry for 1-2 minutes, or until wilted and tender. Add the fish sauce, sugar and salt to taste.

Serve with steamed rice or as an accompaniment to a main meal.

Sri Lankan ONION SAMBAL

MAKES 340 G (12 OZ/1 CUP)

20 g (¾ oz) tamarind pulp, soaked in 1½ tablespoons boiling water (or use 3 teaspoons tamarind paste)

100 ml (3½ fl oz) vegetable oil

1 cinnamon stick

10 cloves

2 star anise

1 sprig curry leaves

1 pandan leaf, tied in a knot

6 large red onions, thinly sliced

3 tablespoons Dried chilli powder (see page 209)

sea salt, to taste

1 tablespoon coconut sugar

Very similar to an onion relish, this traditional Sri Lankan dish goes with everything. We love it as a side with pressed coconut rice, but it also goes fantastically well with bread. Try it and see how easily it fits in with your favourite recipes.

Use your fingers to squeeze the tamarind to separate the flesh from the seeds. Pour the tamarind mixture into a sieve set over a bowl to catch the pulp. Using your hands or a spoon, stir and press to extract as much tamarind pulp as possible. Discard the fibres, membranes and seeds left in the sieve and set the pulp aside.

Heat the oil in a large frying pan over medium–high heat, add the cinnamon, cloves and star anise and fry for a few seconds. Add the curry leaves and pandan leaf and toss in the pan. Add the onion and sauté for 4–6 minutes, or it becomes translucent. Add the chilli powder, salt and 3 teaspoons of the reserved tamarind pulp and cook, stirring, over low heat for 20–25 minutes, or until the onion breaks down and has a jammy consistency.

Add the coconut sugar and cook for 5–10 minutes, or until the onion mixture is caramelised.

Fish out and discard the cinnamon, cloves, star anise, curry leaf sprig and pandan leaf. Store the sambal in an airtight container in the fridge for up to 2 weeks or in the freezer for up to 6 months.

Four Kinds of MUSHROOMS with BLACK PEPPER

2 tablespoons canola oil

3 garlic cloves, finely chopped

50 g (1¾ oz) fresh black fungus

50 g (1¾ oz) king brown mushrooms, sliced

50 g (1¾ oz) fresh shiitake mushrooms, sliced

50 g (1¾ oz) shimeji mushrooms, separated

1½ teaspoons coarsely ground black pepper

½ teaspoon sea salt

1 tablespoon oyster sauce

½ teaspoon sugar

Even more than the way it tastes, I love the way this dish *feels* – sort of velvety and crunchy at the same time. It's packed full of goodness and makes a great accompaniment to main meals. The varieties of mushrooms listed here are my preference, but of course you can use whatever combination you like.

Heat a large wok over high heat and add the oil until it is slightly smoking. Add the garlic and stir vigorously until it just becomes golden – be careful not to let it burn otherwise it will taste bitter.

Add the black fungus first, then the king brown, then finally the shiitake and shimeji, and toss to combine.

Pour in 60 ml (2 fl oz/¼ cup) of water and add the pepper, salt, oyster sauce and sugar. Stir-fry until the mushrooms are slightly wilted, then serve immediately.

DESSERTS

We don't often have dessert after a meal but we do enjoy sweets at other times of the day: with a mid-morning cup of tea, as an afternoon snack, even for breakfast! Treat yourself, but do it in moderation. Remember that with rich, creamy desserts a little goes a long way.

Deep-fried BANANA DOUGHNUTS

400 g (14 oz) very ripe
(almost black) lady finger
bananas

1 tablespoon sugar
(optional, depending on
the sweetness of the bananas)

50 g (1¾ oz/¼ cup) rice flour

50 g (1¾ oz/⅓ cup) plain
(all-purpose) flour

¼ teaspoon sea salt

¼ teaspoon baking powder

vegetable oil,
for deep-frying

You're going to love this tea-time delight! The recipe calls for very ripe
bananas, so if you have any that look like they're going to combust, this
is the perfect way to use them up. The doughnuts are best enjoyed with
a cup of tea or coffee.

Mash the bananas in a medium bowl and add sugar to taste. Add the
flours, salt and baking powder and stir well.

Pour the oil into a medium saucepan to a depth of 10 cm (4 inches) and
heat to 180°C (350°F), or until a cube of bread dropped in the oil browns
in 15 seconds.

Scoop heaped tablespoons of batter into the hot oil, but don't overcrowd
the pan. Work in batches of three or four doughnuts at a time. The batter
will sink, then float to the surface. Fry for 4–5 minutes, turning once or
twice, until the doughnuts are dark golden and cooked through. Transfer
to a wire rack and repeat with the remaining batter. Serve immediately.

MORE PLEASE!

BUCHE de NOEL

5 egg whites

130 g (4½ oz) caster sugar

9 egg yolks

85 g (3 oz) plain
(all-purpose) flour

RUM SYRUP

65 g (2¼ oz) caster
(superfine) sugar

1 tablespoon rum

CHOCOLATE BUTTERCREAM

180 g (6½ oz) caster
(superfine) sugar

100 g (3½ oz) 70% dark
chocolate, plus extra shaved
chocolate to decorate

2 eggs

2 egg yolks

¼ teaspoon sea salt

300 g (10½ oz) unsalted
butter, diced and softened

This log is a very traditional Christmas dessert in France. During the festive season, the pastry shops are full of them in all different flavours and often topped with a lot of tacky plastic decorations! But it really doesn't matter whether you dress it up or down – this chocolate cake is to die for.

Preheat the oven to 220°C (425°F) and line a 40 cm x 30 cm (16 inch x 12 inch) baking tray with baking paper.

For the rum syrup, combine the sugar and 125 ml (4 fl oz/½ cup) of water in a clean saucepan and bring to the boil over high heat. Stir until the sugar has completely dissolved, then reduce the heat and simmer for 3 minutes. Pour the syrup into a heatproof bowl or jug and set aside to cool to room temperature before adding the rum.

Put the egg whites in the bowl of an electric mixer fitted with a whisk attachment and whisk to soft, foamy peaks. Gradually add 50 g (1¾ oz) of the caster sugar, beating until stiff peaks form.

Put the egg yolks in a second bowl with the remaining caster sugar and whisk for 4–5 minutes, or until very pale and creamy.

Fold one-third of the egg white meringue into the egg yolk to loosen the mixture, then gently fold in the remaining meringue – you want to keep the mixture fluffy but make sure no streaks of egg white remain. Sift over the flour in two batches, gently folding it into the batter until nicely combined.

Spread the batter evenly into the prepared baking tray and bake for 5–6 minutes, or until pale golden. Remove and allow the cake to cool in the tray. When cool, flip the sponge over onto a new piece of baking paper and carefully peel the old paper off. Set aside.

For the buttercream, combine the sugar and 250 ml (9 fl oz/1 cup) of water in a clean saucepan and boil for 15–20 minutes, or until the syrup has reduced, is just starting to change colour and registers 118°C (235°F) on a sugar thermometer.

While the syrup boils, break the chocolate into pieces and put it in a heatproof bowl over a saucepan of simmering water, taking care that the base of the bowl does not touch the water. Gently stir until melted, then set aside to cool to room temperature.

In a large bowl, whisk the eggs, egg yolks and salt with electric beaters for 3 minutes, or until thick and pale. When the syrup reaches 118°C (235°F) quickly dip the bottom of the saucepan into cold water to stop the syrup cooking further. Slowly pour the syrup into the egg mixture, beating at a high speed as you pour. Continue beating for 10–12 minutes, or until the mixture doubles in volume and cools to room temperature. Reduce the speed to medium and slowly add the butter cube by cube, beating until the buttercream becomes very thick. If the mixture looks a bit curdled

simply keep beating! Add the melted chocolate and beat until well combined. Scoop one-third of the mixture into a separate bowl.

To assemble the buche de noel, place the sponge cake lengthways on the bench in front of you, keeping the baking paper underneath. Use a pastry brush to soak the sponge with the rum syrup, then spread the reserved third of the buttercream evenly over the entire cake.

With a long side closest to you, and with the help of the baking paper to make sure it's nice and tight, carefully roll up the sponge to create a roulade. Roll the paper around the roulade and place it on a baking tray, seam side down. Refrigerate for 2 hours.

Remove the roulade from the fridge. Cut a 5 cm (2 inch) slice from each end and reserve to use as the 'knot wood' decoration. Place the centre piece of cake on a serving platter and cover with most of the remaining buttercream. Place one reserved slice on the top of the roulade at one end, and the other slice at the opposite end, facing the other direction. Cover the new additions with the rest of the buttercream, keeping the roulade swirls visible on each piece. Finally, use the tines of a fork to create a texture in the cream that resembles the bark of a tree.

The buche de noel can now be stored in the fridge, but you will need to take it out about an hour before serving so the buttercream can return to room temperature. Decorate with chocolate shavings and/or your favourite Christmas decorations before serving. This is best eaten within a day or so of making.

CHOCOLATE *and* CHILLI CRÈME BRÛLÉE

SERVES 6

1½ sheets gold-strength gelatine leaves

5 egg yolks

100 g (3½ oz) caster (superfine) sugar, plus 2 tablespoons extra

¼ teaspoon espelette chilli powder

400 ml (14 fl oz) thin (pouring) cream

2½ tablespoons full-cream (whole) milk

60 g (2½ oz) 70% dark chocolate, coarsely chopped

Who doesn't love a classic crème brûlée, and who doesn't love chocolate? And we all know that chocolate and chilli make an exciting combination, so imagine putting all three of them together in one very sexy dessert! Espelette is a little town in the Basque country that is very famous for its chillies. If you can't find this particular type, substitute with regular chilli powder or cayenne, if preferred.

Cover the gelatine leaves with cold water and set aside for 5 minutes to soften.

In a large mixing bowl, vigorously whisk the egg yolks, sugar and half the chilli powder until pale yellow and very creamy.

Pour the cream and milk into a saucepan over high heat and bring just to the boil. Remove the pan from the heat and slowly pour into the egg yolk mixture, whisking constantly to incorporate. Tip the combined mixture back into the saucepan, reduce the heat to medium–low and cook, whisking constantly, for 1–2 minutes, or until the custard just begins to boil.

Take the pan off the heat. Squeeze the gelatine leaves with your hand to remove any excess water and whisk into the custard. Add the chocolate and whisk again until melted and smooth, then stir in some or all of the remaining chilli powder, to taste.

Press the mixture through a fine sieve, then pour evenly into six shallow 125 ml (4 fl oz/½ cup) ramekins. Refrigerate for a minimum of 2 hours, or until set.

Just before serving, sprinkle a layer of the extra caster sugar over each set custard and shake gently to even it out. Using a kitchen blowtorch, melt the sugar until it turns to caramel, then let it set for a few minutes to harden to a glass-like finish. If you don't have a blowtorch, melt the sugar under a hot grill (broiler). Serve immediately, otherwise the caramel will start to soften.

Traditional Basque ALMOND CREAM and CHERRY JAM CAKES

SERVES 8

200 g (7 oz) unsalted butter, softened

170 g (6 oz) caster (superfine) sugar

100 g (3½ oz) almond meal

1 egg

1 egg yolk

½ teaspoon dried yeast

300 g (10½ oz/2 cups) plain (all-purpose) flour

pinch of sea salt

1 quantity Crème pâtissière (see page 204)

110 g (3¾ oz/⅓ cup) cherry jam, plus extra to serve

icing (confectioners') sugar, for dusting (optional)

FRANGIPANE

100 g (3½ oz) unsalted butter, softened

100 g (3½ oz) caster (superfine) sugar

100 g (3½ oz) almond meal

1 egg

My best friend Jean-Francois Salet is from Pau, a beautiful town in the Basque country, and owns a quaint little restaurant, Le Pelican, in Sydney. He shared this recipe with me and it was so yummy that I had to share it with you.

Put the butter, sugar, almond meal, egg, egg yolk and yeast in the bowl of an electric mixer with a paddle attachment and beat until smooth and well combined.

Sift together the flour and salt, then gradually add to the mixture, a little at a time, until the flour is just incorporated. Turn out the dough onto a lightly floured surface and knead gently with the palm of your hand until just combined. Shape the dough into a ball, wrap in plastic wrap and refrigerate for 1 hour before using.

For the frangipane, combine all the ingredients and beat until smooth. Beat in the cooled crème pâtissière.

Preheat the oven to 160°C (315°F). Grease eight 10 cm (4 inch) loose-bottomed fluted tart tins.

Remove the dough from the refrigerator, cut into four portions and roll out on a lightly floured surface to a thickness of 4 mm (3/16 inch). From the rolled dough cut out eight 12 cm (4½ inch) rounds and eight 10 cm (4 inch) rounds.

Place the larger rounds in the prepared tart tins, leaving a small lip all the way around. Evenly divide the frangipane mixture among the tarts, filling the cases to about two-thirds full. Make a small teaspoon-sized well in the centre and drop 1 teaspoon of cherry jam into each. Place the small pastry rounds on top of each tart case and seal the edges.

Bake for 30–35 minutes, or until crisp and golden.

To serve, remove the tarts from the tins and dollop an extra teaspoon of jam in the centre of each one. Dust with icing sugar, if desired.

OMELETTE SOUFFLÉ *with* BERRIES

6 egg yolks

80 g (2¾ oz) caster (superfine) sugar

4 egg whites

pinch of sea salt

20 g (¾ oz) butter

icing (confectioners') sugar, for dusting

BERRY COMPOTE

100 g (3½ oz) cherries, halved and pitted

100 g (3½ oz) strawberries, hulled and quartered

100 g (3½ oz) raspberries

100 g (3½ oz) blueberries

2 teaspoons caster (superfine) sugar

30 g (1 oz) butter

1 tablespoon brandy

Definitely one to make when you want to impress your friends – easier than a soufflé but just as light, sweet and delicious. If you can, make it when fresh berries are in season but you can substitute with frozen if fresh are unavailable. And because this is all about the lightness of a soufflé, it should be made with organic or free-range eggs.

Preheat the oven to 180°C (350°F).

To make the berry compote, place a large frying pan over medium–high heat, add the fruit, sugar and butter and cook for 5 minutes, or until the fruit is soft and the juices have started to thicken. Pour in the brandy and flambé. To do this, light a long match and ease it down to the surface of the liquid, without actually touching it. Remove the match as soon as the alcohol ignites and allow it to burn off. Transfer the compote to a bowl and set aside to cool slightly.

Put the egg yolks and 1 tablespoon of caster sugar in a large bowl and whisk for 2 minutes, or until the mixture is thick and pale.

Put the egg whites and salt in a second bowl and whisk with electric beaters until foamy. Slowly add the remaining sugar and beat to glossy soft peaks.

Fold one-third of the egg white meringue into the yolk mixture to loosen it. Add the remaining egg whites in two batches, gently folding to combine.

Place a 20–22 cm (8–8½ inch) non-stick ovenproof frying pan over low heat, add half the butter and heat until just foaming. Pour in half the egg mixture and shake the pan gently to spread it out. Cook for 5 minutes, then transfer to the oven to bake for 3 minutes, or until puffed and lightly golden.

Spoon half the berries over one side of the omelette, run a spatula around the edge and fold it in half to enclose the filling. Slide it onto a large plate.

Wipe out the pan and repeat with the remaining butter, egg mixture and compote to make a second omelette (stir the egg mixture once or twice beforehand to ensure an even texture). Slide the second omelette onto the other half of the serving plate.

To serve, dust with icing sugar and cut into wedges.

Chocolate PARIS-BREST

MAKES 8

3 eggs

50 g (1¾ oz) caster (superfine) sugar

30 g (1 oz) cornflour (cornstarch)

250 ml (9 fl oz/1 cup) full-cream (whole) milk

90 g (3¼ oz) Nutella

1 quantity Choux pastry (see page 205)

1 egg yolk whisked with 1 tablespoon milk

50 g (1¾ oz/⅔ cup) flaked almonds

125 g (4½ oz) unsalted butter, softened

50 g (1¾ oz) icing (confectioners') sugar, plus extra for dusting

These choux pastry rings are traditionally filled with a simple hazelnut buttercream. It's hard to improve on perfection, but I kept going back to the idea of including Nutella in the filling and had to try it. So good! The recipe is a little labour-intensive perhaps but it is most definitely worth the effort. If you have any choux batter and filling left over, pipe it in small dollops in any unused spaces on the baking trays. When baked and cool, slice them nearly all the way through the centre and fill with any remaining Nutella cream. These can rightfully be regarded as the cook's treat.

Whisk the eggs and caster sugar in a large bowl for 1 minute, then whisk in the cornflour until smooth. Pour the milk into a medium saucepan and bring to a very gentle boil over medium heat. Slowly pour the hot milk into the egg mixture, whisking constantly. Tip the custard back into the saucepan and cook for 2–3 minutes over medium heat, whisking constantly until very thick. Stir in the Nutella, then transfer to a bowl and press plastic wrap directly on the surface to prevent a skin from forming. Refrigerate for at least 1 hour, or until cold.

Preheat the oven to 200°C (400°F). Line two baking trays with baking paper and use a pencil to draw four 6 cm (2½ inch) rounds on each sheet of paper, giving a total of eight rounds. Flip the paper over so the pencil is on the underside but the lines show through.

Spoon the choux pastry batter into a large piping bag fitted with a plain 1 cm (½ inch) nozzle. Pipe the pastry into a circle over one of the pencilled lines. Pipe another circle on the outside of the first, just touching but not overlapping. Finally pipe a third circle on top of the seam between the bottom two circles. Repeat with the remaining batter and pencil circles until you've piped all eight rings. Carefully brush the pastry rings with the egg yolk mixture, and scatter with flaked almonds.

Bake for 15 minutes. Reduce the oven temperature to 180°C (350°F) and bake for a further 10 minutes, or until golden and the pastry sounds somewhat hollow when tapped. Turn the oven off, prop the door open slightly, and leave the pastry to dry out and cool completely.

To finish the filling, beat the softened butter with the icing sugar for 5 minutes, or until very pale and creamy. Remove the cold Nutella custard from the fridge, stir to loosen a little, and then fold it into the buttercream. Spoon into a piping bag fitted with a 1 cm (½ inch) star nozzle.

Carefully slice the pastry rings in half horizontally. Pipe a generous amount of the Nutella cream onto the bottom halves, then put the top halves back on, dust with extra icing sugar and serve immediately.

GLUTINOUS BLACK RICE
with COCONUT

SERVES 4

300 g (10½ oz/1½ cups)
black glutinous rice

2 pandan leaves,
tied into a knot

110 g (3¾ oz/½ cup)
white sugar or coconut sugar

375 ml (13 fl oz/1½ cups)
coconut cream

½ teaspoon sea salt

In Clarissa's family, this is usually served for 'tea', which in Malaysia means an afternoon snack. I find it very difficult to say no as this is one of my favourite Malaysian sweet dishes. I particularly love the luscious texture of the black rice combined with the coconut cream – just writing about it is making me crave it!

Put the rice in a sieve and wash under running water a couple of times to remove any excess starch.

Put the pandan leaves, rice and 1.5 litres (52 fl oz/6 cups) of water in a medium saucepan and bring to the boil, then reduce the heat slightly and slow-boil for 35–40 minutes. Add the sugar, then reduce to a simmer and cook, partially covered, for 40–45 minutes, or until the rice grains have split open and the rice is tender. The liquid in the pan will have thickened to the consistency of a light syrup. Towards the end of the cooking time, stir the rice to prevent it from scorching and sticking to the bottom of the pan.

Meanwhile, combine the coconut cream and salt in a small saucepan over low heat. As soon as it comes to a simmer, remove the pan from the heat and set aside. You don't want to let the mixture boil.

Ladle the rice pudding into serving bowls and drizzle the coconut cream over the top. Serve immediately. Any leftover pudding will keep in a covered container in the fridge for up to 1 week. Reheat gently before serving.

Sugee CAKE

500 g (1 lb 12 oz) butter, diced and softened

300 g (10½ oz) caster (superfine) sugar

300 g (10½ oz) fine semolina

160 g (5¾ oz) slivered almonds

15 egg yolks

1 tablespoon brandy

1 tablespoon vanilla essence

80 g (2¾ oz) plain (all-purpose) flour

1 teaspoon baking powder

2 egg whites

If you ever been to a Eurasian wedding or a special occasion in Malaysia, you're likely to have been offered a slice of this cake. It's somewhat like a butter cake but every family guards its recipe like diamonds in a vault! It can be made as a light or dense cake – this one is the light version. A friend of Clarissa's family (Aunty Esther Lee) kindly gave this recipe to Clarissa's mother, with no arm twisting required. And yes, it does contain 15 egg yolks – it's not a typo!

Place the butter and half the sugar in the bowl of an electric mixer and beat on high for 2–3 minutes, or until pale and fluffy. Add the semolina and beat for another minute until well combined. Cover with a damp cloth and set aside for 3–4 hours.

Toast the almonds in a dry frying pan over low heat for 2–3 minutes, or until a pale-golden colour. Finely chop and leave to cool to room temperature.

Preheat the oven to 160°C (315°F). Grease a 22 cm (8½ inch) springform cake tin and line the base with baking paper.

In a clean bowl, beat the egg yolks and remaining sugar on medium for 4–5 minutes, or until very thick and pale. Add to the semolina mixture and beat for another 3–4 minutes.

Beat in the brandy and vanilla until smooth. Beat in the sifted flour and baking powder until combined, then stir through the chopped almonds.

In a separate bowl, whisk the egg whites to soft peaks. Fold one-quarter of the egg whites into the semolina mixture to loosen it, then fold in the remaining whites, taking care not to knock out too much air.

Dollop the batter into the prepared tin and smooth the surface with an offset palette knife or crank-handled spatula.

Bake for 35–40 minutes, or until a skewer inserted in the centre comes out clean. Cool in the tin for 10 minutes before turning out onto a wire rack to cool completely. Store in an airtight container for up to 10 days.

TAPIOCA PUDDINGS
with PALM SUGAR CARAMEL SAUCE

MAKES 4

400 g (14 oz/2 cups) sago (tapioca seeds)

1 egg white

2 pandan leaves

125 ml (4 fl oz/½ cup) coconut milk

pinch of sea salt

100 g (3½ oz) gula melaka (dark palm sugar), shaved

You'll often see this dish on Malaysian menus, and on our dining table at home! It really only has three main ingredients, and the rest are included to enhance the flavour and texture. Pandan is the vanilla of Malaysian cooking and adds a distinctive flavour and aroma. The leaves are available fresh or frozen from Asian food stores.

Place the sago in a fine sieve and rinse under running water for 10–15 seconds to remove any excess starch.

Bring 2 litres (70 fl oz/8 cups) of water to the boil in a large saucepan and add the rinsed sago. Cook, stirring constantly, over high heat for 10–15 minutes, or until the sago balls become translucent.

Drain in a large sieve, then use a wooden spoon to stir the sago pearls under running water for about 30 seconds, or until the starch separates and the water runs clear. (You may need to do this in three or four batches.) Tip the rinsed pearls into a large bowl. Whisk the egg white to soft peaks and fold it through the sago to loosen it.

Scoop the sago pearls into four 250 ml (9 fl oz/1 cup) serving dishes and place in the fridge to chill.

Wash the pandan leaves and tie in a loose knot. Place in a saucepan with the coconut milk and salt and bring to a simmer over medium heat. Remove from the heat, strain into a bowl and set aside to cool to room temperature.

Meanwhile, put the gula melaka and 2 tablespoons of water in a small saucepan and melt over low heat. Set aside to cool.

Serve the tapioca puddings with a drizzle each of palm sugar syrup and infused coconut milk.

THIN APPLE *and* ALMOND TARTS

SERVES 4

2 pink lady apples

1 teaspoon lemon juice

1 x 375 g (13 oz) roll of Carême puff pastry, thawed in the fridge (or if you have time, make your own — see page 205)

15 g (½ oz) unsalted butter, melted

1–2 tablespoons caster (superfine) sugar

vanilla ice cream, to serve (optional)

CALVADOS FRANGIPANE

100 g (3½ oz) unsalted butter, softened

150 g (5½ oz) caster (superfine) sugar

1 egg

1 egg yolk

100 g (3½ oz) almond meal

30 g (1 oz) plain (all-purpose) flour

1½ tablespoons Calvados (apple liqueur)

I must have made thousands of these in my early days as a chef, and no wonder. The buttery puff pastry is topped with a luscious almond cream and thinly sliced apple, then baked until crisp and caramelised. Served with a simple scoop of vanilla ice cream, it's hard to imagine a more delicious dessert.

Preheat the oven to 180°C (350°F) and line a large baking tray with baking paper.

For the frangipane, place the softened butter and sugar in the bowl of an electric mixer with a paddle attachment and beat until pale and fluffy. Beat in the egg and egg yolk, then vigorously stir in the almond meal, flour and Calvados until smooth. Set aside.

Peel the apples, then cut them in half and carefully remove the core. Cut into very thin slices (about 2 mm/¹⁄₁₆ inch thick if you can) and put in a bowl with the lemon juice and 500 ml (17 fl oz/2 cups) of cold water. Stir once, then drain the apple slices on a clean tea towel (dish towel).

On a lightly floured surface, roll out the pastry to create a larger rectangle. Using an 18 cm (7 inch) side plate or ring mould as a guide, cut two rounds from the pastry. Place the rounds on the prepared baking tray and prick all over with a fork to stop it puffing up too much. Any remaining pastry can be pressed back together, wrapped in plastic wrap and stored in the fridge for another use.

Evenly spread 1–2 heaped tablespoons of frangipane on each pastry disc. Any leftovers will keep in an airtight container in the fridge for up to a week, or in the freezer for up to 6 months.

Arrange the apple slices in a concentric circle on top of the frangipane, overlapping to create a flower shape, and place two or three half-slices in the middle to finish. Brush the apple with melted butter and sprinkle with half the caster sugar.

Bake for 10 minutes, then remove from the oven and sprinkle with the remaining sugar. Return to the oven and bake for a further 10 minutes, or until the pastry is puffed in the centre and the apple slices are pale golden.

Serve hot or warm with a scoop of vanilla ice cream, if desired.

APPLE Turnovers

2 tablespoons honey

6 pink lady apples, peeled, cored and cut into small chunks

50 g (1¾ oz) caster (superfine) sugar

2 eggs

2 tablespoons milk

2 x 375 g (13 oz) rolls of Carême puff pastry, thawed in the fridge (or if you have time, make your own — see page 205)

icing (confectioners') sugar, for dusting (optional)

The French are well known for their sweet pastries, particularly croissants and pain au chocolat. Apple turnovers (Chaussons aux pommes) are another favourite. These parcels of flaky puff pastry filled with sweet apple compote were a great treat for us as kids after school, but they are also lovely for dessert, served with a scoop of your favourite ice cream.

Drizzle the honey into a saucepan over medium-high heat and cook until it starts foaming, then add the apple and caster sugar and reduce the heat to medium. Cover and cook gently for 15-20 minutes. Mash the apple with a fork, adding 1-2 tablespoons of water to help soften it. Set aside to cool.

Crack the eggs into a small bowl and whisk in the milk to make an egg wash. Reserve.

Lay one sheet of pastry on a floured work surface and cut out four 12 cm (4½ inch) discs. Repeat with the second sheet of pastry to make eight discs in total. Roll out each disc a little to form an oval shape, ensuring the thinnest end of each oval is closest to you, and brush the edges with some of the egg wash. Place one-eighth of the apple compote on one half of each pastry oval, then fold the other half over the filling to enclose, gently pressing the edges together to seal. Place the pastries on a baking tray lined with baking paper and rest in the fridge for an hour or so.

Preheat the oven to 200°C (400°F).

Brush each turnover with egg wash and decorate the top by cutting shallow incisions in either a fan pattern or parallel lines with the back of a knife. Bake for 20-25 minutes, or until the pastry is golden, crisp and nicely puffed. Cool to room temperature before indulging. Dust with icing sugar, if you like.

Traditional Brittany
BUTTER CAKE

350 g (12 oz) salted butter,
diced and softened

300 g (10½ oz) caster
(superfine) sugar

1 vanilla bean,
split and seeds scraped

7 egg yolks

350 g (12 oz/3 cups) plain
(all-purpose) flour

pinch of sea salt

1½ tablespoons dark rum

jam, to serve (optional)

Butter cake is sold at every little market in Brittany, including the village where my mother lives. The village market is held every Sunday and as a child I always made a beeline for a slice of this cake. It's so beautiful and buttery, and totally melts in your mouth. It's up to you which jam you serve it with – my personal favourite is raspberry, but it also goes well with apricot, blackcurrant, strawberry or black cherry jam.

Preheat the oven to 160°C (315°F) and grease a 24 cm (9½ inch) loose-based tart tin.

Put the butter and sugar in the bowl of an electric mixer with a whisk attachment and cream until light and fluffy. Add the vanilla seeds and six egg yolks (reserve one for the egg wash) and beat until well aerated and pale. Add the flour and salt and beat until just combined, then fold in the rum.

Transfer the batter, which will be very thick, to the prepared tin and pat it down with your hand. Refrigerate for 10–15 minutes.

Remove from the refrigerator. Lightly beat the remaining egg yolk and brush over the top of the cake batter, then use the tines of a fork to mark with a crisscross pattern. Bake for 50–55 minutes, or until the top is golden brown and the edges pull away slightly from the side.

Cool for a few minutes before removing from the tin. Enjoy warm with your favourite jam, if desired. The cake will keep in an airtight container for up to 5 days.

FRIED BANANA *Fritters*

4–6 just-ripe bananas

1 egg

100 g (3½ oz/½ cup)
rice flour

50 g (1¾ oz/⅓ cup)
plain (all-purpose) flour

½ teaspoon baking powder

½ teaspoon sea salt

¼ teaspoon ground turmeric

125 ml (4 fl oz/½ cup)
chilled water

750 ml (26 fl oz/3 cups)
vegetable oil

1 tablespoon melted butter

ground cinnamon and
caster (superfine) sugar,
for dusting (optional)

Because these fritters are such a much-loved snack you'll find 'pisang goreng' vendors everywhere in Malaysia. Clarissa's mum makes them occasionally with tiny bananas called 'pisang emas', which are extremely sweet. This recipe is made with regular bananas sold at local fruit and veg shops, so it's not quite as sweet. The dusting of sugar and cinnamon to finish is optional – totally up to you!

Peel the bananas, cut them in half widthways and then in half again lengthways so each banana is cut into four long pieces.

Place the egg, flours, baking powder, salt, turmeric and chilled water in a medium bowl and mix well. The batter should be slightly thicker than pancake batter.

Pour the oil into a medium heavy-based saucepan or wok and heat to 190°C (375°F), or until a cube of bread dropped in the oil browns in 10 seconds.

Stir the melted butter into the batter, then coat the banana pieces in the batter, allowing any excess to run back into the bowl. (If the batter is too thick, add a little extra water, 1 teaspoon at a time.) Working in batches, carefully drop the battered banana into the hot oil and cook for 2–3 minutes, or until golden brown. Remove with a slotted spoon and drain on paper towel.

Serve immediately, dusted with cinnamon and caster sugar (if using).

MORE PLEASE!

Kouign AMANN

400 g (14 oz) chilled butter, cut into four 1 cm (½ inch) thick slices

300 g (10½ oz) caster (superfine) sugar, plus extra for dusting

2 teaspoons fine sea salt

DOUGH

500 g (1 lb 2 oz/3⅓ cups) plain (all-purpose) flour, plus extra if needed

2 teaspoons fine sea salt

15 g (½ oz) fresh yeast or 1½ teaspoons dried yeast

1 teaspoon caster (superfine) sugar

The kouign amann is very traditional to Brittany. It's pretty much a bread dough that is folded like puff pastry layered with butter and sugar, then baked in the oven. The fluffy, crispy, caramelised result is to die for with a mug of hot chocolate!

To make the dough, put the flour and salt in the bowl of an electric mixer fitted with a dough hook. Combine the yeast, sugar and 400 ml (14 fl oz) of warm water in a small bowl then, with the mixer running at the lowest speed, pour it into the flour mixture and mix until incorporated. When the mixture begins to form a dough increase the speed to high and beat for 8-10 minutes, or until very smooth and elastic. The dough is ready when it doesn't stick to the side of the bowl and pulls any excess dough on the side into itself. If the dough is still a little wet, reduce the speed, add an extra 1–2 tablespoons of flour, increase the speed and beat again. Repeat until the dough is the correct consistency. Transfer the dough to a buttered metal bowl, cover with plastic wrap and sit in a warm spot for an hour, or until the dough has doubled in size.

Turn out the dough onto a floured board or bench and punch down to knock out any air. Knead for 10–20 seconds (or for 12 folds), then roll out to form a 2 cm (¾ inch) thick rectangle. Place the butter slices over two-thirds of the pastry, covering the middle and one side. Fold the uncovered side over the middle with the butter, then fold the side with the butter over that. Rotate the dough a quarter turn, roll out to 1 cm (½ inch) thick and fold again. Repeat this process once more, then cover with plastic wrap and rest in the fridge for 1–2 hours. This gives the dough time to settle and the butter time to harden, which helps retain the layers you are folding in.

Preheat the oven to 200°C (400°F). Grease 16 x 125 ml (4 fl oz/½ cup) muffin holes and dust with sugar. Tap to remove any excess sugar. (If you just have one muffin tin, make them in two batches.)

Combine the sugar and salt.

Roll out the dough to a 2 cm (¾ inch) thickness and sprinkle with about one-sixth of the sugar and salt mixture. Roll it into the pastry and fold in thirds again (as above). Repeat this process three more times.

Roll out the dough to a 1 cm (½ inch) thickness, sprinkle with half the remaining sugar and salt mixture and roll it into the pastry. Flip and repeat on the other side. The pastry should now be a 40 cm (16 inch) square. Cut it into 16 x 10 cm (4 inch) squares, bring each of the corners into the middle and press them into the prepared muffin holes, using your fingertip and thumb to crinkle the sides up.

Bake for 25–30 minutes, or until crisp and very golden. Allow to cool for 1 minute before turning out onto a wire rack to cool. Don't wait much longer than a minute as they are super sticky and will stick to the tin. If this happens, return to the oven for a few minutes to heat up, then flip them out. Serve warm or at room temperature. These are best eaten on the day of baking, but any leftovers may be warmed through in a 180°C (350°F) oven for a few minutes before serving.

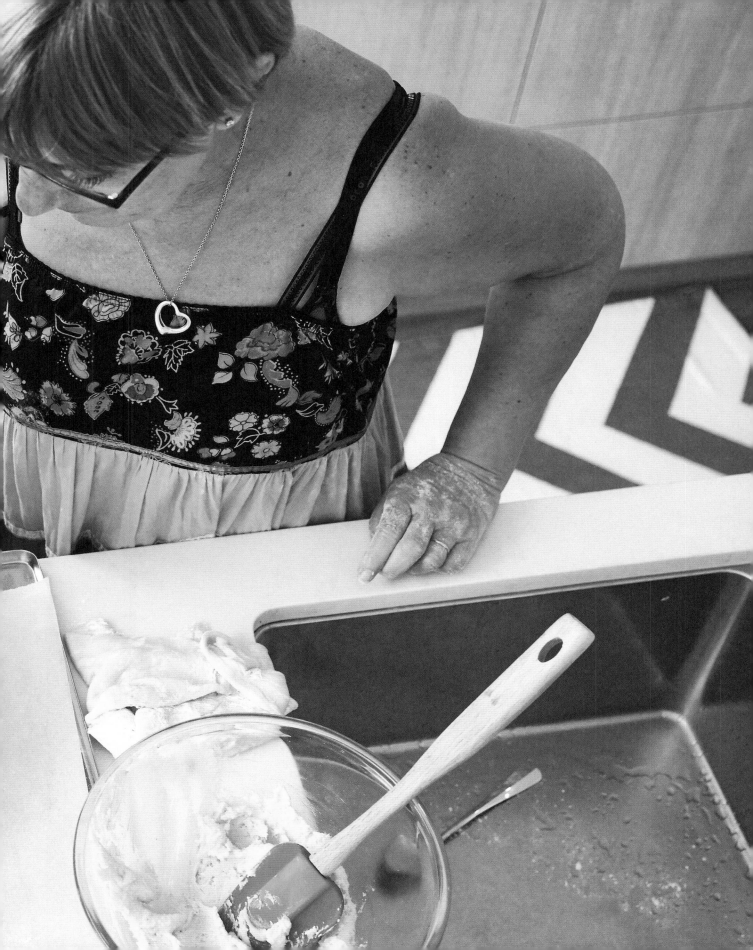

BASICS

It's really straightforward: make it yourself.
It's just better!

Chicken STOCK

1 kg (2 lb 4 oz) chicken
bones, rinsed well

3 litres (105 fl oz/12 cups) water

1 carrot, diced

1 brown onion, diced

1 small leek, pale part only,
well washed and finely chopped

1 celery stalk, diced

1 garlic clove, crushed

1 bouquet garni (see note)

Place the chicken bones and water in a large heavy-based saucepan or stockpot. Bring to the boil over medium heat, skimming any impurities from the surface. Add the carrot, onion, leek, celery, garlic and bouquet garni and return to the boil. Reduce the heat to low and simmer for 3 hours, skimming regularly.

Strain the stock through a fine sieve sitting over a large bowl and discard the solids. (To keep the stock as clear as possible, do not press on the solids when straining.) Cool to room temperature, then refrigerate until cold. The fat will solidify on top of the stock, making it easy to remove and discard.

Refrigerate for up to 7 days or freeze for up to 3 months. (A good tip is to freeze the stock in ice-cube trays so you can take out only as much as you need.)

NOTE : A bouquet garni is a bundle of herbs tied together with kitchen string that usually includes parsley, thyme and a fresh bay leaf (plus sometimes a strip of lemon or orange zest), used to add flavour to soups, braises or stocks. My standard bouquet garni consists of two thyme sprigs and a fresh bay leaf, wrapped in a piece of the green part of a leek, then tied with kitchen string.

MORE PLEASE!

Brown Chicken STOCK

1 kg (2 lb 4 oz) chicken
bones, rinsed well

1 carrot, diced

1 brown onion, diced

1 celery stalk, diced

100 g button mushrooms

500 ml (17 fl oz/2 cups)
dry white wine

2.5 litres (87 fl oz/10 cups)
water

1 garlic clove, crushed

1 bouquet garni
(see note, facing page)

2 tomatoes,
halved widthways

Preheat the oven to 200°C (400°F).

Place the chicken bones in a roasting tin and roast, stirring from time to time, for 30 minutes. Add the carrot, onion, celery and mushrooms to the tin and stir to mix well, then roast for another 30 minutes, or until the vegetables are golden. Transfer the bones and vegetables to a large heavy-based saucepan or stockpot and reserve the roasting tin.

Place the roasting tin over medium heat. Add the wine and scrap with a wooden spoon to remove any cooked-on bits. Pour the wine mixture over the bones, then add the water. Place the pan over high heat and bring to the boil, then skim any impurities from the surface. Add the garlic, bouquet garni and tomatoes, then reduce the heat to low and simmer for 4 hours, skimming the surface regularly.

Strain the stock through a fine sieve sitting over a large bowl and discard the solids. (To keep the stock as clear as possible, do not press on the solids when straining). Cool to room temperature, then refrigerate until cold. The fat will form on top of the stock, making it easy to remove and discard.

Refrigerate for up to 7 days or freeze for up to 3 months. (A good tip is to freeze the stock in ice-cube trays so you can take out only as much as you need.)

Beef STOCK

1 kg (2 lb 4 oz) beef bones

1 carrot, diced

1 brown onion, diced

1 celery stalk, diced

100 g (3½ oz) button mushrooms, quartered

500 ml (17 fl oz/2 cups) dry red wine

2.5 litres (87 fl oz/10 cups) water

1 garlic clove, crushed

1 bouquet garni (see note, page 196)

2 tomatoes, halved widthways

Preheat the oven to 200°C (400°F).

Place the beef bones in a roasting tin and roast, stirring from time to time, for 30 minutes, or until browned. Add the carrot, onion, celery and mushrooms to the tin and stir to mix well, then roast for another 30 minutes, or until well browned.

Transfer the bones and vegetables to a large heavy-based saucepan or stockpot and reserve the roasting tin.

Place the roasting tin over medium heat. Add the wine and scrape with a wooden spoon to remove any cooked-on bits. Pour the wine mixture over the bones, then add the water. Place the pan over high heat and bring to the boil, then skim any impurities from the surface. Add the garlic, bouquet garni and tomatoes, then reduce the heat to low and simmer for 4 hours, skimming the surface regularly.

Strain the stock through a fine sieve sitting over a large bowl and discard the solids. (To keep the stock as clear as possible, do not press on the solids when straining). Cool to room temperature, then refrigerate until cold. The fat will form on top of the stock, making it easy to remove and discard.

Refrigerate for up to 7 days or freeze for up to 3 months. (A good tip is to freeze the stock in ice-cube trays so you can take out only as much as you need.)

Fish STOCK

1 kg (2 lb 4 oz) white fish heads and bones

100 ml (3½ fl oz) dry white wine

3 litres (105 fl oz/12 cups) water

1 brown onion, diced

1 small leek, pale part only, well washed and diced

1 small fennel bulb, diced

1 garlic clove, crushed

1 bouquet garni (see note, page 196)

Remove the gills and any bloodlines from the fish heads and bones and rinse well under cool running water. Place the bones in a large heavy-based saucepan or stockpot, then add the wine and bring to the boil over high heat. Add the water and return to the boil. Reduce the heat to low, then add the onion, leek, fennel, garlic and bouquet garni and simmer, skimming the surface regularly, for 20 minutes, then remove from the heat.

Strain the stock through a fine sieve sitting over a large bowl and discard the solids. (To keep the stock as clear as possible, do not press on the solids when straining). Cool to room temperature.

Refrigerate for up to 7 days or freeze for up to 3 months. (A good tip is to freeze the stock in ice-cube trays so you can take out only as much as you need.)

French DRESSING

1 teaspoon hot dijon mustard

60 ml (2 fl oz/¼ cup) red wine vinegar

sea salt and freshly ground black pepper

200 ml (7 fl oz) extra virgin olive oil

Place the mustard, vinegar and a pinch each of salt and pepper in a small bowl and whisk to combine well. Whisking constantly, gradually add the olive oil in a thin, steady stream until emulsifed.

Vinaigrette can be stored in a sealed glass jar or bottle in the fridge for up to 2 weeks.

Walnut VINAIGRETTE

2½ tablespoons white wine vinegar

1 teaspoon dijon mustard

sea salt and freshly ground white pepper

2½ tablespoons vegetable oil

100 ml (3½ fl oz) walnut oil

Place the vinegar, mustard and a pinch each of salt and pepper in a small bowl and whisk to combine. Whisking constantly, gradually add the oils in a thin, steady stream until emulsified.

Store in a sealed glass jar or bottle in the fridge for up to 1 week.

MORE PLEASE!

MAYONNAISE

MAKES ABOUT 300 G
(10½ FL OZ/1 CUP)

1 egg yolk

1½ tablespoons
dijon mustard

sea salt and freshly
ground white pepper

250 ml (9 fl oz/1 cup)
grapeseed oil

1 teaspoon lemon juice,
or to taste

Place the egg yolk, mustard and a pinch each of salt and pepper in a bowl and whisk to combine well. Place the bowl on a tea towel (dish towel) to help stabilise it as you whisk. Whisking constantly, add the oil, drop by drop at first, then in a slow, steady stream until the mixture is thick and emulsified. Whisk in the lemon juice and adjust the seasoning. If the mayonnaise is too thick, whisk in a little boiling water.

Mayonnaise can be stored in an airtight container, closely covered with plastic wrap, in the fridge for up to 1 week.

AÏOLI

MAKES ABOUT 450 G
(1 LB/1½ CUPS)

1 small floury potato
(about 125 g/4½ oz),
scrubbed

5 garlic cloves,
peeled

sea salt

2 egg yolks

1 teaspoon lemon juice,
or to taste

250 ml (9 fl oz/1 cup)
olive oil

pinch of cayenne pepper

Preheat the oven to 200°C (400°F).

Prick the potato all over with a fork, then place it directly on an oven rack in the centre of the oven and bake for 35–40 minutes, or until cooked through. Remove from the oven and, when cool enough to handle, scoop out the flesh and discard the skin.

Place the garlic and a large pinch of salt in a mortar and pound with a pestle until a paste forms. (Alternatively, finely chop the garlic, sprinkle over the salt and, using the flat side of a kitchen knife, rub the salt into the garlic to form a paste.) Transfer the garlic paste to a food processor, then add the egg yolks, lemon juice and 30 g (1 oz) of the potato and process until smooth. With the motor running, gradually add the oil, drop by drop at first, and then in a slow, steady stream until the mixture is thick and emulsified. Season to taste with salt, cayenne pepper and a little more lemon juice if needed.

Aïoli can be stored in an airtight container, closely covered with plastic wrap, in the fridge for up to 3 days.

Manu
201

Beurre BLANC

3 golden shallots,
finely chopped

60 ml (2 fl oz/¼ cup)
dry white wine

1½ tablespoons
white wine vinegar

1½ tablespoons thin
(pouring) cream

250 g (9 oz) unsalted
butter, chopped and
slightly softened

lemon juice, to taste

sea salt and freshly
ground white pepper

Place the shallot, white wine and vinegar in a small saucepan and simmer over low heat for 4–5 minutes, or until the liquid has reduced to about 1 tablespoon. Whisk in the cream, then reduce the heat to as low as possible.

Whisking constantly, add one piece of the butter at a time, whisking until the sauce is creamy and emulsified; be careful not to boil the sauce at all or it will split.

Strain the sauce through a fine sieve into a bowl, discarding the solids. Add lemon juice and salt and pepper to a taste. The sauce is best served immediately, but will keep in a warm, not too hot, spot near the stove for up to 1 hour.

Clarified BUTTER

350 g (12 oz) unsalted butter

Place the butter in a heavy-based saucepan over low heat and allow it to melt. Simmer until the milk solids separate and fall to the bottom of the pan. Skim away any solids that foam on the top and pour the clear butter into an airtight container, discarding the milk solids.

Clarified butter will keep in the fridge for up to 1 month.

Basic BÉCHAMEL

40 g (1½ oz) unsalted butter

40 g (1½ oz) plain
(all-purpose) flour

500 ml (17 fl oz/2 cups)
full-cream (whole) milk

Place the butter in a medium saucepan over medium heat. When it starts to foam, stir in the flour and cook for 1–2 minutes, whisking regularly. Reduce the heat to low, pour in half the milk and whisk vigorously to stop any lumps forming. Whisk in the rest of the milk and cook for 5–6 minutes, or until the mixture comes to the boil and the flour cooks out.

If not using immediately, transfer the béchamel to an airtight container and cover the surface closely with plastic wrap. Refrigerate until required.

Crème PÂTISSIÈRE

250 ml (9 fl oz/1 cup)
full-cream (whole) milk

1 vanilla bean,
split and seeds scraped

3 egg yolks

50 g (1¾ oz) caster
(superfine) sugar

20 g (¾ oz) plain
(all-purpose) flour

Pour the milk into a saucepan over medium–high heat, add the vanilla seeds and pod and bring to just below the boil. Remove from the heat. Strain through a fine sieve into a jug and set aside to cool.

Whisk the egg yolks and sugar until thick and pale, then whisk in the flour. Whisk in the warm milk until well combined. Pour the custard into a non-stick saucepan and stir over medium–low heat for 2–3 minutes, or until the mixture comes to the boil, then continue to whisk for a further 2–3 minutes until thick and smooth.

Transfer to a cold bowl, and cover closely with plastic wrap to prevent a skin from forming. Leave to cool to room temperature, then refrigerate until cold.

Choux PASTRY

2½ tablespoons full-cream (whole) milk

100 g (3½ oz) unsalted butter

1 scant tablespoon caster (superfine) sugar

pinch of sea salt

150 g (5½ oz/1 cup) plain (all-purpose) flour

4 eggs

Place the milk, butter, sugar and salt in a saucepan over high heat. Add 200 ml (7 fl oz) of water and bring just to the boil, ensuring the butter has melted, then reduce the heat to low. Add the flour and stir vigorously with a wooden spoon to incorporate it into the liquid – the mixture will become very thick very quickly. Continue to stir over low heat for 5–7 minutes, or until the flour is cooked out, and the mixture pulls away from the side of the pan and becomes smooth and glossy.

Allow to cool for 10 minutes. Add the eggs one by one, beating with the wooden spoon to fully incorporate each egg before adding the next. Allow to cool completely, then transfer to an airtight container until needed.

Puff PASTRY

300 g (10½ oz/2 cups) plain (all-purpose) flour

1 teaspoon fine sea salt

300 g (10½ oz) butter

120 ml (4 fl oz) chilled water

juice of ½ lemon

Sift the flour and salt into a bowl. Rub in 100 g (3½ oz) of the butter using your fingertips, then pour in the water and lemon juice and cut with a flat-bladed knife until the mixture starts to form a dough. Tip out onto a lightly floured surface and knead until smooth, then shape into a ball. Cut with a cross in the centre, then cover with a clean tea towel (dish towel) and leave in a cool spot to rest for 10–15 minutes. Shape the remaining butter into a rectangular block.

Open the dough so it resembles a four-leaf clover and place the butter in the centre. Fold the pastry back over to encase the butter. Roll into a rectangle around 2 cm (¾ inch) thick, then fold into thirds and roll again. Fold into thirds again, make a quarter turn and roll. Fold one more time, then wrap in plastic wrap and rest for 30 minutes.

Roll, fold and turn the pastry another six or seven times, then cover in plastic wrap and rest for 30 minutes. Roll, fold and make a quarter turn another two or three times, then cover in plastic wrap and rest for 15 minutes.

Use the pastry straight away or store it in the fridge or freezer. If storing it in the fridge, remove it 5–10 minutes before using, and allow 30–40 minutes to thaw if storing it in the freezer.

Cooked Sambal CHILLI

MAKES ABOUT 300 G
(10½ OZ/1½ CUPS)

125 g (4½ oz) dried long
red chillies

boiling water, for soaking

2 red Asian shallots

½ small red onion

3–4 garlic cloves,
peeled and left whole

2 teaspoons belacan
(dried shrimp paste)

¼ teaspoon sea salt

1 teaspoon sugar

60 ml (2 fl oz/¼ cup)
canola or vegetable oil

Soak the chillies in boiling water for at least 30 minutes. Drain well and put in a food processor or blender with all the remaining ingredients, except the oil. Blend until finely ground.

Heat the oil in a wok or large frying pan over medium-low heat. Add the chilli paste and sauté for 30-40 minutes, or until very fragrant.

Spoon into a sterilised jar (see note). Store in the fridge for up to 4 weeks or freeze in portions and thaw as required. The paste may be seasoned with more sugar, salt, soy sauce or fish sauce, depending on the dish.

NOTE: To sterilise jars, preheat the oven to 140°C (275°F). Wash the jars in hot, soapy water, and rinse well. Place the jars on a baking tray or in a roasting tin and put them in the oven for 10–15 minutes to dry completely.

Sambal BELACAN

MAKES ABOUT 200 G (7 OZ/¾ CUP)

15 g (½ oz) belacan
(dried shrimp paste)

6 fresh long red chillies,
coarsely chopped

2 fresh bird's eye chillies

juice of 1 lime

sea salt and sugar,
to taste

Toast the belacan in a dry frying pan for a couple of minutes.

Using a mortar and pestle, pound the chillies and belacan until it becomes a rough paste, then add lime juice, salt and sugar to taste.

Transfer to an airtight container. The sambal will keep in the fridge for 7 days and up to 3 months in the freezer.

Dried CHILLI POWDER

MAKES ABOUT 500 G
(1 LB 2 OZ)

**500 g (1 lb 2 oz) dried long
red chillies, seeded**

Using a pair of kitchen scissors, roughly chop
the chillies. Wash them in cold water, then rinse
well and spread over a baking tray in a single
layer. Place in a warm safe spot with lots of
sunlight and dry in the sun for a few days, or
until they are very dry.

Transfer to a mortar and pestle and grind to
a very fine powder. Transfer to sterilised jars
(see note, facing page) and keep in a cool dry
place for up to 3 months.

Laksa PASTE

12 red Asian shallots,
peeled

1 x 5 cm (2 inch)
piece turmeric

1 x 7.5 cm (3 inch)
piece galangal

8 lemongrass stems,
pale part only

20–30 g (¾–1 oz)
dried chillies,
soaked in hot water
for at least 30 minutes

12 candlenuts

8 garlic cloves,
peeled and left whole

20 g (¾ oz) belacan
(dried shrimp paste)

1 tablespoon sea salt

1 teaspoon caster sugar

80 ml (2½ fl oz/⅓ cup)
peanut or canola oil

Put the shallot, turmeric, galangal, lemongrass, dried chillies, candlenuts, garlic, belacan, salt and sugar in a blender and pulse to form a smooth paste, adding a bit of water if necessary.

Heat a wok over high heat and pour in the oil. When smoking, add the laksa paste and sauté over medium–low heat for 20–25 minutes, or until fragrant and the oil has split from the paste. Transfer to an airtight container and store in the fridge for up to 10 days or in the freezer for up to 3 months.

Ginger JUICE

250 g (9 oz) ginger

Finely grate the ginger into a bowl covered with a piece of muslin (cheesecloth), making sure you catch all the juices.

Take up all the sides of the muslin and squeeze out as much juice as possible into the bowl. Transfer to a small jar, seal and store in the fridge for up to 7 days.

MORE PLEASE!

Glossary

Aniseed
Not to be confused with star anise, aniseed adds a warm, liquorice flavour to sweet and savoury dishes. For best results, buy the seeds whole and grind them as needed.

Banana leaves
Typically used for cooking, wrapping and serving food on, banana leaves are flexible and waterproof. They impart a subtle sweet flavour to food that is cooked or served on them, but they are not edible and should be discarded after use.

Belacan
Pronounced blah-chan, belacan is fermented shrimp paste sold in a block. Its pungent flavour is a key element in Malaysian cooking and it should be used in small quantities. It is usually roasted before use.

Brik pastry
Brik is a very thin pastry, similar to filo, but with a less flaky texture. It is most commonly used to make savoury or sweet parcels that are baked or deep-fried until golden. Look for it in Middle Eastern or specialist food stores.

Candlenuts
Candlenuts are hard, oily fruit that are often ground and used as a thickening agent in Malaysian cooking. Because they can be slightly toxic raw, they are always cooked before being eaten. Buy them in Asian or Indian food stores. May be substituted with macadamias, if unavailable.

Chinese rice wine
Known as shaoxing, this traditional wine made from fermented rice is used as a cooking wine, usually in meat dishes, and also as a beverage enjoyed at the beginning of a meal. It is available from most Asian grocers but, if necessary, you can substitute it with a dry sherry or Japanese sake.

Chinese sausages (lap cheong)
These are hard cured sausages, usually made with pork and pork fat and flavoured with soy sauce and spices. They must be cooked before eating, usually steamed or stir-fried. Available in Asian food stores.

Chinese five-spice powder
This blend of star anise, cloves, cinnamon, fennel and sichuan pepper is typically used in Chinese cooking but you'll also find it in other Asian and Middle Eastern cuisines.

Coconut sugar
Made from the sap of the coconut palm, coconut sugar is a common sweetener in south and south-east Asian cooking. It is available from Asian food stores and you can also find it in larger supermarkets.

Crispy fried shallots
These thin slices of red Asian shallots are deep-fried until golden and used as a garnish. Crispy fried shallots can be found in Asian grocers or in the Asian aisle of larger supermarkets. Store them in the freezer.

Curry leaves
Curry leaves are dark, shiny, fragrant leaves similar to bay leaves but with a distinctive curry flavour. Buy them fresh or frozen from Asian food stores.

Curry powder
This spice mix is widely used in south-east Asian cuisine. Blends can vary a great deal so, if you can, look for our favourite brand, Babas, which can be found in most Asian grocers. Otherwise, any other traditional mix from Malaysia or south-east Asia should make a good substitute.

Dried anchovies (ikan bilis)
These are salted and sun-dried anchovies used to add flavour and texture to various south-east Asian dishes. Available from Asian grocers.

Dried prawns
Dried prawns are tiny, sun-dried, salted prawns (shrimp), which are valued in Asian cuisine for the umami flavour they impart. They are sold in packets in Asian grocery stores and are different from the slightly larger frozen dried prawns.

Fermented black beans
These little beans are nuggets of pure umami. Made by fermenting and salting black soy beans, they have a sharp, pungent and spicy scent, with a salty, sweet and somewhat bitter flavour. Found in jars or tins, they are available at most Asian grocers.

Fish balls
Fish balls are made with pounded (rather than ground) fish and have a very different texture from western meatballs. Their neutral fish flavour makes them a versatile addition to dishes such as soups and stir-fries. Buy them from the refrigerated section of Asian food stores.

Fishcake
Somewhat similar to fish balls, fishcake is a processed seafood product, where various white fish are puréed, combined with simple seasonings such as salt, formed into loaves and steamed until firm. Find them in the fridge section of your local Asian grocery store.

Galangal
This funny-looking root is from the ginger family and, although it may look similar to ginger, the flavour it imparts is quite different and you wouldn't generally substitute one for the other. It is more fibrous with a distinct pink tinge and is used in most Asian cuisines.

Glutinous rice flour
Glutinous rice flour has a sticky glue-like quality and is very different from rice flour. It is typically used to

make a resilient, flexible dough or pastry or as a thickener for soups and stews.

Ginger cake

Otherwise known as pain d'espices or spice bread, this is used in both sweet and savoury recipes in French cuisine. Traditionally made from rye flour, dark buckwheat, honey and spices, the dough was originally left to ferment before baking to rise, but these days baking powders are added. It can be found in most traditional French bakeries but may be substituted with ginger loaf cake if you can't find it.

Karamel masakan

Made from molasses and salted, this dark caramel sauce is a kind of savoury version of treacle. Look for it in Asian grocery stores or in the Asian pantry section at major supermarkets.

Palm sugar
(gula melaka or gula jawa)

Palm sugar is a dark, unrefined sugar from the sap of sugar palm trees. It is widely used in south-east Asia, not only in sweet dishes, but also to balance the flavours in savoury dishes. Nyonya and Malaysian cuisines usually favour a darker version (gula melaka). Buy it in jars or blocks from Asian food stores.

Pandan

The vanilla of Malaysia, pandan leaves are added to hot liquid to infuse their flavour and scent. Buy them fresh from Asian grocery stores and freeze any remaining leaves to use in other recipes. Pandan extract can be substituted, if necessary, but look for a clear liquid instead of the green version as it will tint your food green.

Panko breadcrumbs

A Japanese style of flaky, coarse breadcrumb used to coat foods to be deep-fried. Available from larger supermarkets and Asian food stores.

Pearl barley

Pearl or pearled barley is barley that has been processed and polished to remove its hull and bran. It is somewhat similar to wheat, with a mild nutty flavour, and is a nutritious alternative to rice or pasta.

Quark

This unsalted soft white cheese is made by heating soured milk until the desired amount of curdling is achieved, then strained. It's similar to fromage blanc, ricotta or cottage cheese, so if you can't find it, use any of these as a substitute.

Sago (tapioca)

Sago is a starch extracted from various south-east Asian palms, processed into a flour or granulated into little balls called pearl sago. It is most commonly used in Asian coconut milk-based desserts. Buy it from Asian grocery stores.

Speck

Often referred to as Italian speck, this is a type of prosciutto but there are a few different regional varieties including bacon, lardo, pancetta or guanciale and any of these can be substituted for it. Speck is available in the deli section in most major supermarkets and gourmet delicatessens.

Squid ink

This dark liquid is commonly used in pasta and sauces as a food colouring or to enhance a dish with its subtle taste of the ocean. It is available from most fishmongers or gourmet grocers.

Sun-dried olives

As the name suggests, sun-dried olives have been just that – dried in the sun – to enhance their flavour. They are layered with salt, washed and dried before basking in natural sunlight. The result is an intensely flavoured salty olive that is quite

different from a brined olive. They can be found in most gourmet grocers.

Superior rice

As with most foods, rice has certain grades of quality and, as you might expect, superior rice is one of the best: a high-quality rice that will hold its shape and won't break up when cooked. It's perfect for fried rice or other dishes where it might be cooked more than once. It is readily available from Asian grocery stores.

Tamarind

Tamarind pulp can be found in most Asian grocers. It comes in a block and has a thick, pasty consistency with seeds in it. Once opened, it's best to store it in the fridge. You can also get concentrated tamarind paste, which is ready to use. The quantity required will depend on the consistency of the paste – if it is thick and concentrated, start with 1–2 teaspoons and taste.

Tofu

Tofu is a white curd made from soy beans. It has a bland flavour that soaks up the flavours it is cooked with.

Japanese egg tofu is a savoury tofu, made with beaten eggs combined with dashi and steamed in moulds. It has a pale-golden colour and a fuller flavour and texture than silken tofu, due to the egg fat and protein.

Fried tofu (tou foo pok) usually comes in large cubes, and is puffed up with a chewy texture. It is often used in soups.

Vietnamese mint

Also known as hot mint or laksa leaf, Vietnamese mint is not actually a member of the mint family. Its spicy flavour makes a great garnish for soups and salads.

INDEX

ACKNOWLEDGEMENTS

This book is about sharing the love of family food and sharing this with the people you love. To me I like to treat everyone as family and below are some of my 'book family' that have assisted in the writing of this book...

The team at Murdoch Books: Jane Morrow, my publisher, for her vision for this book; Virginia Birch for her support and help; Megan Pigott for her creative eye; Rachel Carter for her editing skills; Trisha Garner for her beautiful design and Kat Chadwick for her wonderful illustrations for the chapter openers.

To my wonderful creative team, Rob Palmer and Michelle Noerianto. Your pictures and styling are amazing but your professional and fun approach make working with you a joy!

To Tiffany Page, for your endless hours at a computer, rewriting and editing recipes and then the further hours at a kitchen bench testing the recipes, I'm so glad you joined our team!

Thanks also to, Jennifer Jenner for all the recipe testing and sometimes just making it work!

A huge thanks to Natalie Penny, as we all know my life without you in it would be a lot more chaotic and obviously disorganised, thank you for being so dedicated to your work and me.

Also thanks to my agent Justine May for your support and continuing to believe in me.

To our families for giving us the background and teaching to many of the basics of these recipes. Also for sharing some secret family recipes and allowing us to share them in this book.

Of course it goes without saying but a big thank you to my darling co-author Clarissa, for being you and a food lover like me. I think it is amazing that you and I have had the chance and opportunity to put our family recipes into book.

And last but by no means least my beautiful children, Jonti and Charlee, always remember everything that we do we do it for you.

Published in 2016 by Murdoch Books,
an imprint of Allen & Unwin

Murdoch Books Australia
83 Alexander Street
Crows Nest NSW 2065
Phone: +61 (0) 2 8425 0100
Fax: +61 (0) 2 9906 2218
murdochbooks.com.au
info@murdochbooks.com.au

Murdoch Books UK
Ormond House
26–27 Boswell Street
London WC1N 3JZ
Phone: +44 (0) 20 8785 5995
murdochbooks.co.uk
info@murdochbooks.co.uk

For Corporate Orders &
Custom Publishing, contact
our Business Development Team at
salesenquiries@murdochbooks.com.au.

Publisher: Jane Morrow
Editorial Manager: Virginia Birch
Editor: Rachel Carter
Design Manager: Megan Pigott
Designer: Trisha Garner
Illustrations: Kat Chadwick
Photographer: Rob Palmer
Stylist: Michelle Noerianto
Production Manager: Alexandra Gonzalez

Text © Manu Fieldel 2016
The moral rights of the author
have been asserted.
Illustrations © Kat Chadwick 2016

Design © Murdoch Books 2016
Photography © Rob Palmer 2016

A cataloguing-in-publication entry is
available from the catalogue of the National
Library of Australia at nla.gov.au.

ISBN 978 1 74336 845 9 Australia
ISBN 978 1 74336 849 7 UK

A catalogue record for this book is
available from the British Library.

Colour reproduction by Splitting Image
Colour Studio Pty Ltd, Clayton, Victoria

Printed by C & C Offset Printing Co. Ltd.,
China

IMPORTANT: Those who might be
at risk from the effects of salmonella
poisoning (the elderly, pregnant women,
young children and those suffering from
immune deficiency diseases) should
consult their doctor with any concerns
about eating raw eggs.

OVEN GUIDE: You may find cooking
times vary depending on the oven you are
using. For fan-forced ovens, as a general
rule, set the oven temperature to 20°C
(35°F) lower than indicated in the recipe.

MEASURES GUIDE: We have used 20 ml
(4 teaspoon) tablespoon measures. If you
are using a 15 ml (3 teaspoon) tablespoon
add an extra teaspoon of the ingredient
for each tablespoon specified.